June 17th '82.

Morels of Cardiff:
the History of a Family Shipping Firm

The author, John Morel Gibbs, grandson of Thomas Morel and John Angel Gibbs.

Morels of Cardiff: the History of a Family Shipping Firm

by John Morel Gibbs

Amgueddfa Genedlaethol Cymru
National Museum of Wales
Cardiff 1982

Contents

Foreword

The Welsh Industrial and Maritime Museum was opened in April 1977 as the second major outstation of the National Museum of Wales. The building stands in the heart of one of the most famous docklands in the world and the new institution has a duty to present in its exhibitions and publications something of the exciting history of the area in which it is located. Cardiff was very much a creation of Victorian enterprise and it was fortunate from Cardiff's point of view that the hinterland to the port became one of the richest coal and iron producing complexes in Britain. No less important in the development of South Wales than the industries in the valleys were the shipowners who were concerned with taking the products of a remarkable industrial region to all parts of the world. The great commercial activity in Cardiff attracted men of vision from many parts of Europe, for although before 1850, Cardiff had a number of shipowners, they mainly operated small sailing vessels concerned principally with the coastal trade. Among the immigrants that came to Cardiff were the Morel Brothers of Jersey who arrived in 1861. They married two Gibbs sisters from Portland, Dorset and with their brother-in-law, John Angel Gibbs, established a shipbroking and shipowning business in Cardiff. The enterprise in Cardiff succeeded to such an extent that the East Dock was known as the 'Morel Dock' and anything up to thirty ships, owned or chartered by them, could be loading at the same time in that dock.

It is an honour for the National Museum to publish a remarkable history of this shipping enterprise written by Thomas Morel's grandson, Dr. John Morel Gibbs of Penarth. The work represents the first of a series of books concerned with the industrial and maritime history of Wales planned by the staff of the Welsh Industrial and Maritime Museum.

J. Geraint Jenkins
Curator,
Welsh Industrial and Maritime Museum

Introduction and Sources

Four strands are prominent in this study of a family Firm: the formative influences on the families, the way the Firm prospered and declined, the fortunes made, and the relationships between the Morel and the Gibbs families. It might be thought that the strands should have been teased out and followed separately from their beginning to their end, but they interrelate and a study of the Firm must deal with the matters as and when they occurred.

It has not been usual in the histories of firms for so much financial information to be disclosed, nor is the present climate too sympathetic to large fortunes. If, however, the Firm's trading had not been profitable it would have ceased to trade and a great many people would have been out of work or would never have obtained work in the first instance.

The study owes its origin to a number of factors. Professor Henry Loyn, formerly of University College, Cardiff, and Patricia Moore, of the Glamorgan Records Office, urged the writer to record his memories of his family before they were forgotten, and these provide the anecdotal and personal strands which are present, particularly in the later chapters. Their inclusion is also justified by Susan Gladys Gibbs's wish that the history of the family should be recorded; having read *The Forsyte Saga* with enjoyment, she saw reflections of it in the story of her own family.

The early records of the Firm that are extant were in the possession of John Morel. As the last Chairman of the Company he had kept the Minute Book of Morel Limited from 1888 to 1947 as well as a number of the early documents. He passed these to the writer some few years before his death. If he had not wanted there to be any record of the Firm he could have destroyed them. He may well not have intended their publication in this form. However, the history of a shipping firm should contain more than a list of the ships owned, the dividends paid or passed and the names of the directors and office staff. Letters and documents, many of the early ones in French, reveal the struggles and the stratagems of the Morels and something of 19th century background against which they built up the Firm.

All the records of the Firm's later transactions and anything that remained in the Company's office were destroyed by Ted Morel some six years after the liquidation of the second Morel Limited in 1957, as is not uncommon practice with company records. It has been necessary to reconstruct the last phase of the Firm's life from the records preserved in Company House and with the help of Alan Roberts, former Director and General Manager, and of Alan Hill, also a former Director and Chartering Manager of Morel Limited. They have also helped the writer to understand the workings of a shipping firm in its daily operations.

Susanna Morel had kept a number of the letters that she had received from her husband Thomas, and these came into the writer's possession through her daughter Gladys, together with the Brackenbury letters. Other letters and additional papers were given to him by Mary Lewin after her father's death. Arthur Morel in Jersey had been a recipient of letters from John Morel when the Morels became interested in their Jersey background and these were given to the writer by his daughter, Mary le Morel.

Gladys Gibbs was a conscientious collector of newspaper cuttings and photographs, and her scrapbook was especially helpful for obituaries and social events, although unfortunately many of the cuttings are undated.

The records of the 1861 and 1871 Census were obtained from the Public Record Office, and the Street Directories of Cardiff gave the addresses of the members of the family at different times. Somerset House provided both details of wills and the figures at which they were proved.

Registers of Shipping contain details of all the Morel ships and the writer first went through these at Lloyds in London and then at the Welsh Industrial and Maritime Museum. Working from this information, Harold Appleyard of the World Ship Society, compiled a complete history of all the Morel ships from their building to the end of their service at sea — this is included as an appendix.

The National Maritime Museum at Greenwich has the originals of the Crew Lists or Agreement and Account of Crew for selected years. A study of these has shown where the Morel crews came from and their wages, and a record of the voyages of the individual ships, the ports visited and the time spent in discharging cargoes.

This information is also contained in an appendix.

The writer consulted the archives in the Cardiff City Hall for records of council meetings and of the complimentary dinner to Thomas Morel, and the back numbers of South Wales papers in the Cardiff Public Library.

The Dowlais Iron Company's collection of letters housed in the Glamorgan Archives contain a considerable number of communications, letters and telegrams from the Morel Firms which documented the scope of their trading and their business methods.

Thomas Morel's grand-daughter, Posy Lewis, and his grand-daughter-in-law, Phyllis Morel, have discussed the Thomas Morel side of the family with the writer. His knowledge of the later history of the Philip Morel family was sparse and it has been possible to fill this in from information received from Philip's grand-daughter, Ursula Warren, and his grand-daughter-in-law, Daphne Morel.

Visits have been paid to Jersey, Portland and Waterford. The writer still lives within four miles of Butetown where the families first made their homes, and knows Cardiff and its environs well.

It is tempting to try to fill in the gaps in the history. The minutes of the annual general meetings of a private company disclose little about that company; the conversations between the members of the family which follow when the meeting is closed reveal more, but are not usually on record. This holds true of Morel Limited and applies to other incidents as well where formal records are tantalizingly brief and unrevealing.

There are a number of surmises which the writer has made about situations and people which may in fact be wrong. For the greater part, however, the facts are firm, and comment and value judgments have been kept to a minimum.

Almost all the people written about in the study are dead and the author hopes that he has dealt fairly with them. No doubt a certain bias in favour of Methodism and against horses is detectable, but the writer hopes that he has been honest, neither concealing the quite remarkable profitability of the Firm, nor passing over the rivalries and quarrels inherent in family businesses — to which the Morels and the Gibbs were by no means immune.

The writer has not discussed his final script with the members of the Morel and Gibbs families still living and he trusts that they will be sympathetic to his publishing material that is usually not disclosed in commercial and maritime biography. They are in no way committed to any of the views expressed.

Acknowledgements

Firstly, I must thank Professor Henry Loyn, who, when he was at University College, Cardiff, stimulated the writing of this book. He also made many valuable suggestions after reading the first draft. Equally, I must thank Patricia Moore for her encouragement and for the very helpful introduction she gave me to the Dowlais Iron Company Records in her care in the Glamorgan Record Office; also, Leslie Jones, a former colleague in the Economics Department of University College and lately of the Welsh Office, for his careful reading of the script and stringent criticisms, which have enabled me to remove some of the infelicities both of content and style.

I must also thank the College of Arms, the Public Record Office, Somerset House, the Archivist at Cardiff City Hall and the Librarian at the Cardiff Central Library for the search facilities made available to me. I was grateful for the opportunity to study the 'Registers of Shipping' both in the Library at Lloyds and at the Guildhall Library, and the 'Agreements and Accounts of Crews' at the National Maritime Museum at Greenwich.

My special thanks to the World Ship Society and especially to Harold Appleyard for his comprehensive study of the Morel ships and their histories.

To Geraint Jenkins and his staff at the Welsh Industrial and Maritime Museum I owe a particular debt, both in the making available of their Library of Lloyds Registers of Shipping and, more particularly, for their encouragement to me to work this history up into a form in which it can be published, and, indeed, for their sponsoring its actual publication.

I owe a debt to Cynthia Randell, who typed my near illegible manuscript and to Marjorie Owen Evans and Joan Dawson who also typed sizeable portions. My gratitude, also, to the still living members of my family for the anecdotes and quotations which appear in the later chapters and especially to Alan Roberts and Alan Hill, the two surviving Directors of the Firm, without whose expert help the two penultimate chapters could not have been written.

Finally, I thank my wife, who worked beside me for many hours in record offices and libraries and on whose sense of good English style I have drawn for many of the more readable prose passages.

CHAPTER ONE

Jersey and Portland

The two families, who together formed the firm of Morels of Cardiff, came from the Islands of Jersey and Portland, making their way by sailing ship to Cardiff in the mid nineteenth century. Although the Firm bore the Morel name from Jersey, the contribution of the Gibbses of Portland was considerable. The two Morel brothers, Philip (1841-1908) and Thomas (1847-1903), who founded the original firm, married two Gibbs sisters, Martha (1844-1933) and Susanna (1843-1910), and took their brother-in-law, John Angel Gibbs (1849-1884), into partnership with them. It was indeed, a family firm.

The history begins with the life on the two Islands and the conditions which prevailed and which led to both families setting out for a new life on the mainland. Because they came from close-knit island communities it is comparatively easy to discover relationships between individuals and families and a Gibbs Pedigree was drawn up in 1927 and a Morel Pedigree in 1936.

Relevant portions of these are reproduced so that it is possible to trace the ancestry and follow the descendants of Philip and Thomas Morel and Martha, Susanna and John Angel Gibbs.

Jersey [1]

Jersey, the largest of the Channel Islands with an area of forty-five square miles, lies within fifteen miles of the French coast. This fact has played an important part from Norman times onwards as the Island provided refuge for those wishing to escape from France at various periods in its history. It would seem that the first Morel came to Jersey from Lisieux as a Huguenot refugee whose brother had been burned at the stake for his Protestant faith.

A farm in the St. Lawrence Parish came into the possession of a descendant, Collas Morel, in 1560 through his marriage with Marguerite Langois who brought it as her dowry. The farm, which became known as Morel Farm, was strongly built and protected with outer walls, being part of the defensive line established in the fifteenth century which stretched across the Island.

In the nineteenth century Jersey was still essentially a land of farmers. Many of the farms were small yet they provided a reasonable livelihood for the farmer and his family. Morel Farm was a typical example with its double roadside arch, horse-drawn cider press, dovecot and piggery. It was, as was customary, a mixed farm which at one time had been considered large, but with many partages had dwindled to a few fields around the farm buildings. There were two or three Jersey cows and the fields grew wheat, swedes, turnips and, inevitably, potatoes. Potatoes had been introduced into Jersey as a field crop in 1815.

Morel Farm in Jersey, now the property of the National Trust of Jersey.

Because of the seaweed, which could be freely gathered from the rocks surrounding the Island and which the farmers used as manure, the soil did not become exhausted and potatoes could be harvested and shipped to Britain before the British crop was ready to be lifted. Potatoes were the only field crop to be so exported, some 4,000 tons a year of the autumn crop being sent to British ports, along with quantities of butter, apples, cider, grapes and oysters.

Morel Farm, as was the case with most of the farms on the Island, was never able to support more than one family and in each generation the younger Morel men had to find their livelihood elsewhere.

In, or about, 1835 Edouard Thomas Morel, a descendant of Collas Morel and nephew to Jean Morel, the then owner of Morel Farm, married Rachel Le Moignan, a member of a long established Jersey family. They lived in the neighbouring parish of Saint Mary and in 1844 built Stuart Farm for their own occupation. The house, of pink granite, characteristic of all the houses of this and earlier periods, was built without the traditional courtyard and the farm buildings were modest in comparison with those of the older farms. The farmhouse itself was commodious enough to accommodate Edouard and Rachel Morel and their three elder sons, Edward Jean, Jean and Philip and the three younger children who were born in the house, Thomas, Elizabeth and Mary. Edward Jean was baptised on 4th January, 1837, Jean on

23rd December, 1838, Philip on 28th January, 1841 and Thomas on 1st June, 1847.

The language of the home was French; Jersey French. Although there is no record of where the elder sons went to school, Thomas received his formal education at Oxenford House, in the neighbouring Parish of Saint Lawrence, where the tuition was in English. He would have walked there daily along the roads protected by banks and hedges against the frequent strong winds. The fees were modest, £1 per quarter for Day Pupils, and the atmosphere stimulating:

> 'No effort is spared to promote the pupils' intellectual achievement. Frequent examinations of all the classes are conducted in order to maintain a spirit of emulation. Constant effort is made to excite a spirit of enquiry and thus to develop the minds of pupils in connection with their daily work . . .'

as ran the prospectus of Oxenford House in the 19th century.

Like many Jersey families the Le Moignans were Wesleyans and the Morel children attended the Sunday School of La Chapelle Bethlehem which had been built in 1829 with an Ecole de dimanche added in 1835. It was there that Thomas Morel was presented with a fine leather bound Bible as a prize on 22nd October, 1858 when he was eleven years old.

Methodism had come to Jersey in 1774 from Newfoundland rather than direct from England.[2] As a consequence of the prosperous fishery trade, many Jerseymen manned the vessels and worked in the cod fishing establishments in and around the mouth of the St. Lawrence river. A missionary who had been influenced by John Wesley's preaching was sent there from England by the Society for the Propagation of the Gospel and converted some of the Jersey exiles. On returning to their homeland they took their Methodist faith and practice with them. Their influence was strengthened by the presence of Methodist soldiers from the regiment stationed in Jersey for garrison duties in 1783, and in the same year Robert Carr Brackenbury, a cultured follower of John Wesley who could speak French, was 'stationed' in the Island.

In August 1787 John Wesley himself visited Jersey, and on the 23rd August, he rode to St. Mary's Parish and preached at Mrs. Le Couteur's house at Le Marais. As not one of his hearers could understand English, the whole service was translated into French. There were a number of Methodist revivals in the early years of the nineteenth century, and the Methodists became one of the leading Churches on the Island.

As Jean, Philip and Thomas began to look to the future, the smallness of Stuart Farm was a factor which they had to take into account. At the present time it consists of 25 vergees, or 10 acres, and was little,if any, bigger in the 19th century. It would be able to provide a livelihood for only one son and this, by tradition, would be the eldest son, Edouard Jean. Primogeniture did not

Stuart Farm in the parish of St Lawrence. Built by Edouard Jean Morel in 1844.

Exporting the potato crop from St Helier, Jersey in 1895.

hold in Jersey and it might seem that the Jersey form of Gavelkind — sharing between the heirs — would provide for the younger sons, but so small were the holdings that a device had to be effected to maintain the farms in any sense as economic units. The eldest male or eldest female inherited the farmhouse with all the appurtanances and a small portion of the land, and then of the remainder two thirds of the land was divided equally between the sons and one third between the daughters. The eldest son, however, then usually purchased back from the others the share of the property that they had inherited, so the other brothers and sisters were provided with a modest amount of capital but no livelihood.

The Island of Jersey likewise provided few openings for younger sons. Other than agriculture there was little but the sea; trade with France, and with Britain, and with Newfoundland. At this time there were many shipbuilding yards along the south coast and a large number of sailing ships traded from St. Helier. The export of Jersey crops was largely in Jersey bottoms. In the 1850s, Philippe Le Moignan, brother-in-law of Edouard Thomas Morel of Stuart Farm, set out for Cardiff to negotiate the sale of the potato crop in the expanding market of South Wales. He sailed to Bristol from St. Helier and then took the boat plying regularly across the Bristol Channel to Cardiff. Philippe Le Moignan was to provide the opening in Britain that his three young nephews, Jean, Philip and Thomas, needed.

Portland

A hundred miles north of Jersey, projecting from the coast of Dorset, is the Island of Portland, a block of solid limestone, four and a half miles long and one and a half miles wide. Although joined to the mainland by the Chesil Bank, Portland was virtually an island. There was no complete road and at the point convenient of access to Weymouth was a tidal inlet, the Fleet, whose strong currents often made the crossing by ferry boat to the mainland difficult and dangerous.

There were few visitors to the Island and few of the Island people ever went to the mainland — even Weymouth might have been a foreign country.

> 'The few strangers who came to Portland were regarded with the deepest suspicion and were known as 'Kimberlins'. Portlanders rarely married anyone from outside the Island. The result of this intermarriage was, of course, to increase the isolation of Portland, and the close inter-relationship of families on the Island. This is to be seen in the comparatively small number of surnames.'[3]

Late eighteenth and early nineteenth century water-colour artists, such as S. H. Grimm, J. W. Upham and John Nixon, in an attempt to attract visitors to Portland, sketched the romantic aspects of the Island, but they were not able to counteract the more general conviction contained in a 19th century guidebook.

'The walk over the top of the Island will introduce the visitor to five of the seven villages. It is hardly possible for human habitation to present collectively a more dreary and unsociable aspect than a Portland village. The houses stand on either side of a wide grass grown road full of ruts and covered with scattered stones. Not a tree or bush is seen, no rural sound is to be heard. The only objects before the traveller are monotonous piles of ragged stone walls, dust heaps and bare rocks.'

Amongst the small number of surnames is that of 'Gibbs', first recorded in 1568. In the early eighteenth century the Gibbses are designated as quarrymen or farmers. Records indicate that they took a prominent part in the representative affairs of the Manor. They could write well at this time when most of those they did business with could only make their marks. William and Benjamin were the favourite male names in the family. The William Gibbs who was born in 1743 married an Elizabeth Elliott in 1770. In 1791 he was a churchwarden and he appears to have been a man of some substance being listed as a freeholder with land valued at a rental of 2/7d, a high figure for 1792. William and Elizabeth had one daughter, Ann, born in 1772 and one son, William, born in 1774.

The Island was not, however, without visitors. Robert Carr Brackenbury, the Methodist gentleman preacher who had returned to England from the Channel Island some few years earlier, was travelling in Dorset: Robert Pearce in his *Methodism in Portland* wrote:

'Shortly after Mr. Wesley's death in 1791, Mr. Brackenbury, suffering from an infirm state of health, partially retired from active labours, and leaving Raithby Hall, sought repose in the south of England. At Weymouth, he was met by Mr. Blunt of Frome who instantly said, "Oh Sir, you are the very person I wanted; the Isle of Portland is all darkness; you must go there".'[4]

Mr. Brackenbury and his young second wife responded to the request and arrived in Portland on 30th October of that year. They had no sooner taken a dwelling house and furnished it comfortably than they used it for preaching and for other religious activities.

Brackenbury's ministry established Methodism securely in Portland and both the young William Gibbs, son of the churchwarden, and his wife, Sarah, became members of the Society. The *Methodist Magazine* for 1861 carried the latter's obituary notice.

'On August 2nd, 1861, died at Portland, Sarah Gibbs, aged 85, relict of Mr. William Gibbs. Among the first fruits of the labours of R. C. Brackenbury, Esquire, in the island, she, with her revered husband, stood the test of the persecution during the stormy days. They ranked also among the closest and latest correspondents of Mrs. Brackenbury.

Mrs. Gibbs became impressed by the truth at the age of seventeen, united herself to the Church in 1793. In 1810 she was appointed leader of a class, which office she filled with fidelity and assiduity, securing the esteem and admiration of those who were entrusted to her care. In her humble cottage the ministers were cheerfully and hospitably entertained, and no visitor received a more hearty welcome. In her deportment she was a fine specimen of primitive godliness — plain in dress, unassuming in carriage, cheerful in disposition, liberal in her acts of kindness, a keeper at home, a peacemaker, yea, an Israelite indeed.'

William Gibbs, too, was a stalwart figure; a trustee of both the Methodist Chapels on the Island, he and his wife became firm friends of the Brackenburys in spite of the considerable difference in social class that separated them, but which their common Methodist faith transcended. In Robert Wiggatt's will of 1809 his son-in-law, William Gibbs, is described as a tailor. Later documents such as Trust Deeds describe him as a farmer, doubtless because he and his wife, Sarah, inherited a number of fields and small holdings from his mother Elizabeth, née Elliot, and from his wife's parents, Robert and Sarah Wiggatt.

As the nineteenth century progressed the isolation of the Island became less and less acceptable even to the Portlanders themselves.

There was a violent storm on the morning of the 23rd November, 1824. John Angel, Master Mariner of Chesil, Portland, so described it in his diary.

'on Tuesday morning about 6 or 7 o'clock a very strong gale S.S.W., the sea came over the Beach and washed down about 25 houses and 75 more filled with beach [pebbles], and greatly damaged. 22 men, women and children killed or drowned.'[5]

This again raised the matter that had been the subject of a petition to King George III and of discussion in the parish meetings from 1776 onwards; the provision of a bridge over the Fleet to supersede the ferry. The ferry consisted of two boats, one for horses, cattle, sheep and goods, and one for foot passengers drawn across by a rope attached to posts at either side of the swift flowing Fleet river.

A temporary ferry was re-established and a committee of the inhabitants of Portland was formed to work for the provision of a bridge. William Gibbs was one of the Commissioners charged in the 1830s with the building of the bridge and it was opened on 31st January, 1839. Although Portland was now joined to the mainland by road, its isolation was still maintained, to an extent, by the stubborn wills of the Islanders and their peculiar beliefs.

One of these was a belief in witchcraft which persisted as late as the year 1816 and which split even the Methodist Society. Many of the Islanders were convinced that every event was regulated by an evil power and every misfortune was attributed to a witch. At the Quarter Session of April 1817 John Flann, aged 20, of Portland was convicted of being 'a Rogue and Vagabond and pretending to crafty science and representing himself as a wizzard to the great disturbance of the peace of the inhabitants of Portland.'[6]

The Rev. Francis Derry, the Methodist minister, had the previous year personally interrogated each member of the Society and if they admitted their belief in witchcraft, he instantly struck their names off the Class Lists. Thus about fifty members, amongst them leaders and local preachers, were turned out of the Society.

> 'The result was the foundation of a new church, which had its centre at Chiswell and ultimately a chapel was built. For years this went by the name of "Conjurers Lodge" and much bitterness of feeling was experienced.'[7]

In 1826 William and Sarah Gibbs with the Rev. James Dunbar attended the Methodist Conference in Bristol in order to bring about a reconciliation between the two Methodist factions in the Island. In this they were successful with the help of Mrs. Brackenbury who provided encouragement—and suitable refreshments — on the occasion of the special leaders' meetings and joint Services.

William and Sarah had four sons but three died in childhood or young manhood. Their surviving son, born in 1812 and also called William, was not strong. Mrs Brackenbury wrote:

> 'he should never lift great weights having ruptured a blood vessel'

She was very solicitous also as to his physical and spiritual welfare:

> 'Is he better? — growing in Grace?'[8]

Mr. and Mrs. Brackenbury returned to Raithby Hall in 1793 but continued to visit Portland almost every year, sometimes travelling all the way in their own carriage. They supported the Methodist Societies in Portland and the poor of the Island and William Gibbs acted as their almoner in distributing their gifts and benefactions. Robert Carr Brackenbury kept up a regular correspondence with the Methodists on the Island, especially with the Minister stationed there, and with William and Sarah Gibbs. On his death in 1818 Mrs. Brackenbury continued the correspondence and the benefactions. William and Sarah Gibbs did not allow these to be one-sided and for their part sent mutton from Portland to Lincolnshire in exchange for gifts of game from Raithby Hall. In his will Robert Carr Brackenbury left William Gibbs his pocket Bible from which he had read his text for his first sermon in Portland.

John Angel of Chisel, or Chiswell, who had recorded the Great Storm of 1824 in his diary, wrote as the first entry:

> 'John Angel came from French Prison in a small boat. May 24. 1812.'

— presumably having been taken prisoner in the Napoleonic Wars. Thereafter his entries alternated between details of storms and shipwrecks and of events in the life of the Methodist Societies, for he, too, was a Methodist. On 24th July, 1837 his daughter Susanna, then aged 21, married William Gibbs, aged 26. They remained on Portland for a year or so.

1838 was an important year in the lives of William and Susanna Gibbs; during it they left Portland and moved to Waterford in Southern Ireland, where they lived for some eighteen years.

The Angel family had established themselves in Waterford as early as 1833 and there are records of the building of schooners of 151 and 181 tons for Angel and Company from that date onwards. The Angels were also listed as sail-makers and ship chandlers supplying the needs of ships and it was in this latter business that William Gibbs was engaged. Gibbs family lore preserved two traditions; that William had 'climbed in through the cabin window', — by marrying the master's daughter his career can be so described, — and that the Angels had originally gone to Waterford for the purpose of carrying stone there for the building of the breakwater. Portland ships sailed to most of the ports of England and Ireland carrying either the highly esteemed building stone or the heavier coarser stone known as roach for such purposes as the building of break-waters, such as was used for the Portland breakwater itself, built between 1849 and 1872 to provide a deep water refuge for the ships of the British Navy.

Between 1790 and 1850, Waterford was an important and thriving port and benefitted from being the last port of call of the ships engaged in the flourish-ing Newfoundland trade. There was a Methodist Society in Waterford. John Wesley had visited Ireland regularly over the years of his ministry and had left a small group of Methodists in that predominantly Catholic area. The Gibbses and Angels attended the Methodist Chapel and their children were baptised there as the surviving Baptismal Register bears witness.

In addition to working as a ship-chandler, William Gibbs also spent some time at sea, and his Master's certificate could be seen for many years in the office of his grandsons' firm, Gibbs and Co., in Merthyr House, Cardiff, until the building was destroyed by fire in 1945. As a further confirmation of this, Mrs. Brackenbury's sister wrote to his parents, William and Sarah Gibbs, in Portland:

> '. . . How delighted we shall be to see Mr. Gibbs [ed: the friend of the Bracken-burys] at Raithby and if he could sail to London with your son, he could come on to Boston by some ship . . .'[9]

This was a somewhat optimistic suggestion as William was at this date in his 73rd year.

After 1850, Waterford gradually ceased to be the important port it once had been. Whilst Susanna Gibbs's brother, Thomas Angel, and his family remained in Waterford as late as 1876, another of her brothers, William Angel, moved to Liverpool and established himself as a shipowner there, and William and Susanna Gibbs, with their seven children sailed for Cardiff some time between 1856 and 1861.

CHAPTER TWO

Butetown, Cardiff

In the early years of the 19th century Cardiff was a small Welsh market town clustered around its Norman castle and St. John's Church, and still almost completely within its mediaeval walls. It was not to remain so for long. Together with some 22,000 acres of land in the mountains and valleys to the north and west of Glamorgan, it formed part of the Bute Estate. The Marquesses of Bute were the landlords of Dowlais, soon to be the site of the world's greatest iron works, and the landlords of the sylvan valleys under which lay extensive seams of the best coal. It needed only an entrepreneur such as the Second Marquis of Bute, who held the Estate from 1814 to 1848 and 'in whom an evangelical sense of duty was combined with an aristocratic high-handedness and ruthlessness worthy of a self-made industrial baron',[1] to enable Cardiff to respond to the logic of the geographical situation.

Workers began to pour into the town from neighbouring counties and further afield. Cardiff ceased merely to be the stopping place on the Romantic Tour of South Wales from which could be visited the ivy-clad ruin of Llandaff Cathedral, and moved towards becoming the 'Coal Metropolis of the World'.[2]

The Glamorganshire Canal and the developing port strove to take the pressure of the great quantities of iron that were being sent down from Merthyr and Dowlais and, in addition, there was the coal.

As the immediate vicinity of Cardiff could not possibly burn all the coal which lay below his lands the Marquis had commissioned a report in 1828 on the state of the harbour at Cardiff, which was, from his point of view, the natural outlet from the coal-fields. This report recommended the building of a new dock parallel to the sea lock at the entrance to the existing, but inadequate, Glamorganshire Canal. Work commenced on the West Dock in 1834 and it was opened in 1839.

However, it was not only ships that needed to be accommodated. In the 1840s Cardiff's old town had become greatly overcrowded and quite unable to provide accommodation for those who were to make their living about the new docks.

> 'The reason for this overcrowding was the great influx of people, especially destitute Irish. These unfortunates poured into Cardiff, brought by sea without payment for their passage from Cork and Waterford by captains who found it easier to load their boats with human ballast than with stones.'[3]

They crowded into the mediaeval courts surrounding St. John's Church and posed a very serious threat to the health of the whole town.

To meet the growing needs of the mid-nineteenth century for urban accommodation and living facilities the Bute Estate planned a model town. Butetown was intended to be largely a self sufficient community distinct from the old Cardiff. The land was leased to builders on terms of 99 years and strict control was exercised over plans and elevation. There were both business and residential areas, the former being near the Pierhead.

> 'Within fifteen years Butetown was virtually completed and had become the main business area of Cardiff, while Bute Street itself had become a fashionable shopping centre. The residential development was laid out on a grid-iron plan and varied considerably in quality from rude cottage terraces to the genteel-rustic terrace of Windsor Esplanade (built about 1850) looking smugly out across the harbour entrance to Penarth Head opposite. In between were two- and three-storey blocks of dwellings, some of which, with their cast-iron balconies, must have once looked quite elegant.'[4]

With Loudoun Square, in which was situated the Wesleyan Chapel, as a focal point and with the Windsor Esplanade as a vantage point from which to watch the shipping in the Penarth Roads, it could be considered a pleasant new town.

The new West Dock and Butetown alongside it, may well have been the talk of those who earned their living by the sea, especially in places like Waterford where trade was beginning to be depressed. In their forties, William and Susanna Gibbs arrived in Cardiff, settling with their seven children in a small cottage-type house at 15 Stuart Street in Butetown. William Gibbs, with his eldest son, William Benjamin, established his ship chandling and sail making business, Gibbs and Company, at 44, Stuart Street, supplying and provisioning the many ships that were beginning to use the Dock. In 1860, of their other children, Susanna was 17, Martha 16, and John Angel and Robert schoolboys of 11 and 5 respectively.

Philip Le Moignan, the Jerseyman, was already established as a potato dealer at 55, St. Mary Street. Cardiff was developing and offering great opportunities in contrast to the Isle of Jersey, and he brought over his young nephew Jean, probably in 1856, to assist him in his business of marketing the Jersey potato crop.

Jean did not remain long with his uncle Philip. The Docks presented many opportunities for a young man. He took advantage of his ability to speak French to enter the chartering business. In October 1861 on an Agreement fixing a uniform tariff for French coasting vessels entering and leaving the port of Cardiff he was described as 'the main British party', although only just twenty years of age. The Agreement noted that 'French Commerce is increasing daily with Cardiff'. The French market had been opened up by John Nixon, the young mining engineer who, from 1840 onwards, introduced Welsh coal to the French naval authorities so successfully that they adopted it as fuel for their ships, and French private shipping concerns generally followed suit. A thriving trade in the export of coal developed between the Welsh and French ports, largely in French sailing ships.

Jean had gone back to Jersey early in 1861 to marry his distant cousin Mary Morel at St. Lawrence, and they returned to Cardiff to 20 Stuart Street. The census of 1861 recorded: Jean aged 22, Mary aged 19, and a young Irish general servant.

Jean sent to Jersey for his two younger brothers to join him in the chartering business, confident that there were almost unlimited opportunities in Cardiff. Philip came to Cardiff in 1861 when he was twenty and later in the year Thomas, who was only fourteen, arrived to join his brothers. They became the 'and Company' on documents — 'John Morel and Company,' with their elder brother, Jean at 2 Stuart Street.

Thomas in his youth was described in his obituary of 1903 as:

> 'always having been an observant young man he quickly became acquainted with the intricacies of the shipping trade . . . at 17 he became a shareholder in a sailing vessel managed by his brother, Mr. Jean Morel.'

The partnership did not last beyond 1866. The brothers saw their futures in different ways. Jean had seized the opportunity of entering the ship chartering trade and his firm had become one of the seven engaged in the export of coal to France and beyond, but he seems to have feared the risks involved in actually owning ships. There was, too, the issue of the importing of iron ore from Spain. Again from the obituary:

> 'Messrs. Morel Bros. must be credited with having imported to Cardiff the first cargo of Iron Ore from Spain. It was brought over in one of their sailing vessels called the Joseph et Marie in 1866. Up to that time British ore had been used in iron making. No one seemed to know anything of Spanish ore, and the cargo remained on the quay for months before anyone would purchase it.'

This story seems to be apocryphal. Iron ore had been imported into Wales considerably earlier than 1866. Cargoes of iron ore may well, however, have been a rare sight on the dockside in Cardiff at the time. Possibly the combination of the move into actual ship owning and the importing of iron ore, with its uncertain market, which doubtless the Firm did early engage in, proved too great a strain for the eldest brother. As his obituary worded it:

> 'Jean elected to accept the agency of the Llynvi Tondu Coal and Iron Company and reside at Porthcawl.'

This was in 1867, the year that the new dock at Porthcawl was opened. The three brothers dissolved partnership. The two younger went ahead on their own as 'Morel Frères et Cie'.

Jean's first child, John Edouard, had been born on 9th July, 1864, and baptised at Loudoun Square Chapel before the move to Porthcawl. Jean did not stay in Porthcawl for more than two years as, when his second daughter, Emily Rachel, was born on 12th August, 1869, the Loudoun Square baptismal register described him as being 'of Cardiff'. The street register gave his address as St. Albans Villa, The Walk, Tredegarville, Cardiff. The move back to Cardiff did not signal a healing of the breach between the brothers. The break remained serious. In his will, Jean did not make either of his brothers his

Executor but appointed William Benjamin Gibbs, whom he would have known through shipping and chapel contacts — a fact which underlined the estrangement.

Nor did Thomas ask him to his wedding some years later. Thomas wrote to him on the actual morning of his marriage a note which Jean kept amongst his papers to his death:

'Morel Frères et Cie
Courtiers Maritimes
Exporteurs de Charbons

Cardiff
le 4 Feb. 1873

Dear Brother,

I fully intended seeing you last night but I had so much to do to have matters put in order that it was quite impossible for me to go up.

By the time this will reach you I will be married. I need not tell you who with.

You have always taken a great interest in my welfare and you will agree with me that it is by far the best course. I hope to be able to walk in the course you have trained me for.

In haste

I remain

Your affectionate brother

Thomas

In the Street Directory of 1875/6 Jean is described as a general merchant of 50 Mount Stuart Square. In addition to his brokerage business he was engaged in the importing of pitwood, largely from Ireland, and in the shipping of some iron. He was prepared to take commissions on a wide scale as, for example, 'French potatoes, vegetables, pitwood and other French produce that might come his way'.

In planning his return to Cardiff he clearly hoped to be able to use 2 Stuart Street as an address for his Agency and was uncertain whether the estrangement would prevent him from so doing. However, in the Street Directory of 1880/1 — some considerable time after his death — we find that the office of the Llynvi Tondu & Ogmore Coal and Iron Company is housed there, so it is not unreasonable to assume that Morel Frères gave him the accommodation he needed in their offices.

His second son, Arthur, was born three months before his death in Cardiff on 14th February 1875.

His estate in Britain was proved for 'under £4,000', a tiny fraction of the amounts his brothers were to leave. There was, in addition, Jersey property which came under Channel Island jurisdiction. His widow, Mary, continued to live in The Walk until her death in 1916.

His eldest son, John, married a Jersey girl, Ida Matzaro, but worked in

Butetown and the West Dock, Cardiff. Stuart Street with the Morel Limited offices runs from left to right.

Cardiff, with the coal exporting firm of Cory Brothers and later, with his uncles in Morel Limited. He was never a partner in the Firm, a position which he might well have held if his father and uncles had remained in business together. It is probable, however, from the character that emerges from his obituary at his death in 1924 that he did not envy his uncles the eminent positions they were to achieve.

> '. . . For many years he was connected with the chartering department of Morel Limited and was a well known figure on 'change. His gracious, kindly manner won for him the respect and regard of all who came into contact with him. Mr. John Morel was not a public man. He avoided everything which would tend to bring him into the limelight . . .'

When he ceased to work in the Firm he retired to Jersey.

His younger brother, Arthur, became a bank manager and he, too, on his retirement settled in Jersey. Thus was severed in the twentieth century the Cardiff connection with the branch of the Morel family which had first pioneered the move there in the nineteenth.

Phillipe Le Moignan also left Cardiff. At the 1871 Census he was living at 8, Stuart Street and had moved his potato store to Pendoylan Street, just north of the West Dock. Sometime after this date, with his wife and three children, he returned to Jersey.

Philip and Thomas Morel remained in Cardiff to exploit the openings he had created for them.

CHAPTER THREE

Morel Frères et Cie

From the obituary of Thomas Morel in 1903:

> 'In 1867, when only 20 years of age, Thomas Morel and his elder brother Philip went into partnership as shipbrokers with offices in Stuart Street and took over the business established by their brother Jean. Thus, when Cardiff had hardly begun to dream of its potentiality as a mineral port, was laid the foundation of their large and lucrative business which pioneered the shipping trade of the town. At this time the export of coal only reached 836,000 tons. Today [1903] it totals nearly 20 million. The East Dock was only partially opened and practically the whole of the coal export business was carried on in the West Dock. In the early stages of their career the brothers carried on their business chiefly in three sailing vessels owned by them and mostly employed in the West Indian and Brazilian trade, but they also acquired shares in a number of sailing vessels under the French flag.
>
> In those early days Swansea possessed some of the finest sailing vessels on the west coast and it was from that quarter that the young Morels met with their chief competition. They devoted the whole of their energies to their business and they prospered. It was by no means an unusual experience for them to charter as many as 20 or 30 vessels a day, and they eventually succeeded in making the Spanish ore carrying trade almost entirely their own.'

This information contained in the obituary would presumably have been obtained from Philip Morel. The Brazilian trade would be the carrying of coal to South America to supply the needs of the railways which were being developed there. The Morel Brothers certainly acquired a number of sailing vessels of their own, but their main thrust at this time was the exporting of coal to France and other European countries. They shared the importing of iron ore from Spain with the slightly older Padstow shipping firm of John Cory and Sons, who set up business in Cardiff in 1872, and they never succeeded, as the obituary claimed, in making it almost 'entirely their own'.

France was a major market for Welsh coal and the French language was widely used in international trading. Because of their fluency in French the Morel brothers had an advantage over their competitors. In the shipping of the coal they used either their own ships, acting both as chartering agents and as shipbrokers providing the ships in which the cargo was to be carried, or as charterers negotiating the Charter Party by which ships of other owners, not infrequently their masters, undertook to carry coal to ports throughout the world. When they fixed their own ships they took the full profit from transporting the coal, when they acted as charterers they shared the profit with the ship's owners.

To bring ore back from Bilbao ships would sail there, either in ballast after having discharged their cargo of coal at another port, or with whatever cargo could be secured by the Master, as the Charter Party laid down 'for the ship's benefit' and not for the benefit of the charterer. They then loaded the ore at the quay in the Bilbao river and delivered the cargo at Cardiff, or at whatever Welsh port the Charter Party specified. Whenever possible, Morel Frères et Cie, in addition to their inward cargo of iron ore, would endeavour to secure an outward cargo, to Bilbao. This is illustrated by the Charter Party of 21st June, 1871 with Messrs. Ibarra and Co. of Bilbao, whereby Morel Frères et Cie undertook to transport five to six thousand tons of coal at 6/- per ton from Cardiff or Newport to the Baracaldo factory in Bilbao itself, from the 1st of July for twelve months.

One of the earliest recorded acts of Morel Frères et Cie was for Philip Morel to take an apprentice on 1st November, 1867. The Form used was the standard one adapted for the particular situation and it illustrated the very strict terms under which an apprentice bound himself to serve his master.

> 'This indenture witnesseth that Samuel Vivian Rowe of No. 60 Elm Street, Cardiff in the county of Glamorgan, son of Peter Rowe of the same place, Master Mariner, by and with the consent and approbation of his said father, doth put himself apprentice to Philip Morel, of Cardiff aforesaid, Ship Broker and Commission Agent, to learn his art and with him after the manner of an apprentice to serve from the first day of November in the year of our Lord one thousand eight hundred and sixty seven unto the full end and term of four years from thence. During which term, the said apprentice his master faithfully shall serve, his secrets keep, his lawful commands every where gladly do. He shall do no damage to his said master nor see to be done of others but to his power shall tell or forthwith give warning to his said master of the same. He shall not waste the goods of his said master nor lend them unlawfully to any. He shall not committ fornication nor contract matrimony within the said term. He shall not play at cards or dice tables or any other unlawful games whereby his said master may have any loss with his own goods or others. During the said term, without licence of his said master, he shall neither buy nor sell. He shall not haunt taverns or playhouses nor absent himself from his said master's service by day unlawfully, but in all things as a faithful apprentice he shall behave himself towards his said master and all his during the said term. And Philip Morel his said apprentice in the art of a ship broker, commission agent etc. etc., which he useth by the best means that he can, shall teach and instruct or cause to be taught and instructed paying unto the said apprentice for his actual work and labour four shillings per week for the first two years of said term; eight shillings per week for the third year and ten shillings per week for the fourth and last year of said term, provided he shall well and faithfully serve his said master. And the said Peter Rowe hereby covenants with the said Philip Morel that the said Samuel Vivian Rowe shall and will well and faithfully serve the said Philip Morel as an apprentice during the said term of four years according to the true intent and meaning of these presents.
>
> And for the true performance of all and every said covenants and agreements either of the said parties bindeth himself unto the other by these presents. In witness whereof the parties above named to these indentures interchangeably have put their hands and seals the thirteenth day of November and in the thirtieth year of the reign of our sovereign lady, Victoria, by the grace of God of the united Kingdom of Great Britain and Ireland, Queen Defender of the Faith

and in the year of our Lord one thousand eight hundred and sixty seven. Samuel Vivian Rowe, Peter Rowe, P. Morel.'

The first extant Bill of Sale for the purchase of a considerable number of shares in a ship by Thomas and Philip Morel, Ship brokers, is dated 8th November, 1869. Ships at this period were divided in 'Sixty Fourths' and the owners of these shares joined in the profits of the voyages, or bore the loss if any should be incurred, in proportion to their holdings. A transaction was entered at the Custom House, Cardiff, whereby Philip and Thomas Morel bought thirty two sixty fourths for £550 in the two masted schooner, the *Ebenezer*. She was built in wood by William Henry Tonkin of Cardiff, 71 ft. long, 18 ft. in breadth, 9 ft. depth in the hold with a registered tonnage of 69 tons. The witness to the Bill of Sale was John Angel Gibbs, clerk, of 44, Stuart Street, Cardiff.

Here is evidence of a business connection between the Morel and the Gibbs families. Philip Morel had married Martha Gibbs, the third of the four daughters of William Gibbs, on September 26th, 1866. Both families attended Loudoun Square Wesleyan Chapel, both had island backgrounds and their businesses complimented each other; the Gibbs ship-chandling store may well at this time have provided services and equipment for the Morel vessels. On their marriage, Philip and Martha had made their home at No. 1 Windsor Esplanade with its extensive view of the shipping in the Penarth Roads and the Bristol Channel.

A month previous to the purchase of the *Ebenezer*, John Angel Gibbs, aged twenty, the second son of William Gibbs left the ship-chandling business and entered into an agreement with his brother-in-law:

'Cardiff, October 11th, 1869.

Memorandum of agreement between Mr. John Angel Gibbs of Cardiff on the one part and Philip Morel and Thomas Morel on the other part.

That the said J.A. Gibbs engages himself to serve the said P. and T. Morel as Cashier and book keeper and in one word make himself generally useful in the business of Ship Brokers etc.

For these services the said P. and T. Morel shall pay the said J.A. Gibbs the sum of one hundred and ten pounds for the first year and one hundred and twenty pounds for every year after during the time he remains in said employ. One month notice to be given and taken on either side. Should the said J.A. Gibbs leave the said employ and open or go into any other employ in the French Caboteur business in the Port of Cardiff within ten years from the date of this agreement the said J. Gibbs shall pay or cause to be paid the said P. and T. Morel the sum of five hundred pounds within one month of entering into such business or engagement.

John A. Gibbs
Philip Morel
Thomas Morel 11.10.69 '

Susanna Gibbs née Angel 1816-1900.

Jean Morel 1838-1875.

Philip Morel 1841-1908.

Thomas Morel 1847-1903.

The two families were thus not only related by marriage; John was now a member of the Morel Firm, howbeit in a very junior position.

The second Bill of Sale extant is for the purchase of the tug, the *Milo*, built in South Shields in 1868. She was a wooden paddle steamer of 70 tons with a single engine of 35 horse power, 86 ft. in length, 17 ft. in breadth and a hold of 9 ft. On 23rd February, 1870 Morel Brothers bought 64/64 shares in her from Thompson Johnson Newton, steam boat owner, William Softley, engineer, and Tom Softley, shipbuilder, for £1,600.

The Morel Brothers were committed to the expansion of their shipowning interests to the extent of allowing it to interfere with their private lives and domestic arrangements. In May 1868 Philip agreed to sell to his brother, Thomas, his house, No. 1 Windsor Esplanade, and to board his brother at the rate of 8/- per week in consideration of Thomas selling his own house and 'throwing the amount into the trade to the mutual benefit of both parties'. Thomas was to enter into possession of the house, when he required it or became a householder.

The money thus raised could well have been used towards the purchase of the *Milo* or the next sailing ship, the *Gertrude*.[1]

The *Gertrude* had been built in Naples. She was a brig of 198 20/100 tons, 89 ft. long, 20 ft. wide and depth in the hold of 13 ft. Now registered at London, she was owned by her Master, W. Sigg, as to 20 of the 64 shares and by three other London shareholders who owned the remaining 44. The sale was negotiated by Captain Valot who arranged her purchase by Morel Brothers for £505 in April 1871, delivery to be in the West Bute Dock in Cardiff. Later 42/64th shares were transferred to Captain Valot, 22 shares remaining with Philip and Thomas Morel. Captain Valot agreed to act as Master and Philip and Thomas Morel as ships husbands. Both parties agreed not to transfer their shares to another person without consent. The transaction reflects the common practice of a master owning a considerable stake in his own ship, for which he had in this case negotiated the purchase. The *Gertrude* was the only ship of this period which Lloyds Register of Shipping actually designated as in the ownership of the Morels.

In August 1873 Morel Brothers and Co. bought the *Maria Needham*[2] of Liverpool from William Cliff and Bernard Hall, who owned 48 and 16 shares of the 64 shares respectively, for £1,800. She had been built at Grimsby in 1858. Before they bought her she had been repaired in 1871 and American Lloyds classified her as A 1: 'This ship has been opened and found free from rot or decay and in every aspect well found and in first class order'. She was a three masted wooden barque of 127 ft. in length, 25 ft. in breadth, depth in hold of 15 ft. and of 354 tons.

Following their usual practice of not owning the whole of a vessel, Morel

Brothers & Co. sold 43 of the 64 shares in the *Maria Needham* to Thomas Hoult and Joseph Milner, both of Cardiff. In February 1873 they bought back these shares for £1,460 — it is probable that there was an agreement that if the shares were ever to be sold they must be offered to the vendors in the first instance. This transaction shows that the ship increased in value from £1,800 in 1871 to £2,175 in two years. In order to pay for the additional shares a mortgage was taken out with the West of England and South Wales District Bank for £1,000. The ship was underwritten by four different firms amongst them being F. Falquet of Bordeaux who underwrote at 8½ % for the sum of Fr.250,000.

In August 1871 Morel Brothers made a loan to the captain of one of the ships they chartered, Paul Le Veux owner of the *Penero* of Bordeaux, a vessel of 196 tons, of two thousand francs, and the captain agreed to pay back three hundred and fifty francs each journey. He named the ship as security and agreed 'to keep her on the sea route from Bilbao to Cardiff or, if the carrying of cargo to France is profitable, from Cardiff to France and from there to Bilbao, or from Cardiff to France and back'.

From 1760 onwards, the Welsh iron industry, centred on Merthyr and the northern outcrop of the South Wales coalfield, had been growing fast and by 1851 970,702 tons of iron were produced annually by the one hundred and sixty four furnaces then in blast. The presence of iron ore at the top of the Welsh valley together with coal and limestone had been the reason for the siting of the furnaces in that part of Britain. The ore, however, had a high phospheric content and even before the development of Bessemer's method of making steel in bulk in 1856, foreign ores were being imported primarily from northern Spain. Bessemer's process heightened the demand for ores that were phospherus free and the trade with Bilbao increased dramatically. It continued even when methods were developed whereby phospheric ores could be used without ill effect in the steelmaking process.

Morel Brothers threw themselves wholeheartedly into the importing of iron ore. In January 1871 in an agreement with the Aberdare Iron Company, they, as shipbrokers, engaged themselves to supply vessels to carry 5,000 to 6,000 tons of iron ore over a six month period from Bilbao to Cardiff at the rate of 10/9 per ton freight less 1¼ % discount payable on each cargo delivered.

To fulfil this agreement they would have needed to provide ships, either in their own or in other ownership, to bring the ore back from Bilbao and arrange for the discharging of the cargo either at a wharf in Cardiff Docks or on the Glamorganshire Canal.

An even bigger venture was their contract with the giant Dowlais Company. The Dowlais Iron Company obtained their ore from exporters in Bilbao and neighbouring ports and they supplemented this by founding the Orconera

Company in 1872 to operate their own mines in the neighbouring mountains. In March 1871 the Dowlais Iron Company made an agreement with Morel Brothers and Company, shipbrokers, whereby the latter undertook 'to charter, use all their influence and employ all means in their power to procure tonnage for the Dowlais Iron Company from Bilbao, Olavergo or San Nicholas to Cardiff, Swansea or Briton Ferry'. Messrs. Morel Brothers agreed to charter at the best condition of freight in their power and in no wise to exceed the current rate without the sanction of the Dowlais Iron Company who agreed to pay them threepence per ton for all tonnage chartered. The total quantity of tonnage for the remainder of 1871 was not to exceed 40,000 tons. The penalty for non performance of the agreement was 'five hundred pounds' — this was altered at the actual signing of the contract to 'unlimited'. Morel Brothers were apparently confident that they would be able to effect enough Charter Parties to enable the contract to be honoured at rates acceptable to the Dowlais Company. By such agreement, the Dowlais Iron Company ensured that sufficient iron ore would be imported for their furnaces, and Morel Brothers and Company received a commission of threepence per ton over and above the normal brokerage of 5% they would have obtained.

An example of this working out can be seen in a letter of 1st May, 1872 to the Dowlais Iron Company from Morel Brothers and Company in which they offered 500 to 1,000 tons of Bilbao ore at 32/6 per ton delivered.

Three Charter Parties for cargoes of iron ore from Bilbao to Welsh ports of this period are extant. They differ in slight particulars, 14, 12 or 10 working days being allowed for loading and discharging. The Charter to be in force for three or five consecutive voyages. The ships were of 340 tons, 121 tons and 107 tons — the last, the *Bonne Union*, being instructed to unload at Porthcawl. Fourteen shillings and sixpence was the agreed freight in all instances.

Morel Brothers and Co. were not long content to remain solely carriers in the iron ore trade. On 27th May, 1876 they themselves bought a quantity of iron ore, about thirteen hundred tons, from the Spanish firm of Aznar, Zubiria & Co. Exporters of Bilbao and Castro at 19/6 per ton to be shipped to the East Dock at Cardiff for use in the Dowlais Iron Works.

It would seem that Morel Brothers went further. If the Dowlais Iron Company could buy a stake in Spanish mines they would do so too, and actually own the iron ore which they would ship back to Cardiff. There is a copy of an agreement, in French, preserved amongst the Company papers dated, Santandes, 31st January 1874. A Monsieur George Thomas Single agreed to buy all the produce of the mines managed by Augustin Toujouse and owned by a consortium in the mountains and villages of Quebedo, Viveday and Guaza. The sellers engaged to deliver at least five hundred tons a month. They agreed to load the ore at the rate of fifty tons a day on sailing ships and at least one hundred tons a day on steam ships. They agreed to load the ships in a navigable and safe berth in the Riviere de St. Martin (Reghejada).

George Thomas Single agreed to pay forty five Reaux per tonne of 1015 kilogrammes, payment to be made when the cargo was delivered and weighed in Britain, either at the railway or at the port of destination. If George Single wished, all the mineral that could be produced would be sold to him and the contract was to be in force for one year and could be extended up to five years on the same conditions. Morel family tradition has asserted that the Morels actually owned mines in the Bilbao region which this Agreement may seem to confirm. However, apart from the existence of this document amongst the Morel papers there is no positive evidence for such ownership and no clear connecting link between George Single and the Morels has been established.

It is not surprising that with the increased activity Philip and Thomas Morel needed assistance and took John Angel Gibbs more and more into their confidence and made him a party to the decisions taken by the Company. He had 'made himself generally useful' — as his contract stipulated — to very good effect. At first he usually signed as 'clerk'. In May 1873, Morel Brothers & Co. were required before the Notary Public in Cardiff to make a payment of £400 to a Bordeaux firm and John A. Gibbs, 'Cashier', answered; 'we refuse to pay it'. On the bills of sale from 1877 onwards, he signed as 'shipowner'.

John Angel Gibbs was then living beside and over the ship-chandling store at 72 Bute Street with his parents, William and Susanna, his two brothers, William and Robert, who were taking increasing responsibility for the ship chandling business, and his two unmarried sisters, Susanna and Anne.

His parents with their younger children were accustomed from time to time to return to Portland where William had a house, 'Rock Cottage' in the main street of Easton. Portland rather than Waterford or Cardiff was where he really felt at home. This property had come to William Gibbs on the death of his widowed mother in 1861. She had been the sole child of her father, Robert Wiggatt, and brought, as has been noted earlier, Portland property to the family.

When her parents were away from Cardiff, their eldest unmarried daughter, Susanna, kept house for her brothers. The 1871 Census records her and her two elder brothers living in Stuart Street with a young maid, Fanny Turner, of Bath.

In 1865, Sarah, the eldest daughter, had married Edward Pearce of Portland and her ill health was another reason for her parents spending long periods on the Island. Letters from the period have survived and reveal a warm close-knit family. From William Gibbs in Portland to his daughter Susanna in Cardiff asking that his wife should come immediately to nurse their daughter Sarah:

Date 1866 (circa)

'I almost fear from the manner of Edward's telegram that Mother [ed: his wife]

Martha Morel née Gibbs 1844-1933.

Susanna Morel née Gibbs 1843-1910.

may have not left; if not, she will please come at once. You know Sarah has been suffering from sickness for some time. She was almost continually sick for twenty-four hours and an attack on the chest brought on confinement. She is very weak. I have seen her this morning; the two doctors have just left and tell us she is better but requires great care . . . of course, there is no one like a mother . . .'.

Again, William Gibbs to his daughter, Susanna, in Cardiff:

Date: some little time before
his death in 1870.

'. . . I am very thankful to find you get on comfortably with your brothers. You can't do too much for them and I trust they will find equal pleasure in endeavouring to repay your kindness . . .'

After three confinements in quick succession, Sarah Pearce died, only one of her children, Edward, surviving her. He was brought up by his grand parents in Portland and later in Cardiff.

The *Western Mail* for 22nd February, 1871 carried the following announcement:

'There was launched from the building yard of Mr. John Batchelor a splendid iron tug . . . She is the property of Messrs. Morel Brothers shipowners and brokers of this town. The christening ceremony was performed by Miss Gibbs.'

Susanna Gibbs was an interesting choice. She was Philip Morel's sister-in-law and John Angel Gibbs's sister. There was clearly a warm relationship between the Morel and the Gibbs families based on John's membership in the Firm, the inter-relationship of a ship chandling with a ship owning business and their Methodist involvement in the life of Loudon Square Chapel.

The close relationship was further cemented when in February 1873 Thomas Morel married Susanna Gibbs at the Chapel. He was twenty-five, she was twenty-nine. His brother, Philip, had moved in October 1872 to his new house, No. 14, Park Place, so that Thomas and Susanna could take possession of No. 1 Windsor Esplanade, Butetown, as the agreement between Philip and Thomas stipulated.

Later in the same year in Portland, John Angel Gibbs married a young Portland girl, Elizabeth Pearce Scriven, and they moved into their first home, eight doors away from Thomas and Susanna, at No. 9 Windsor Esplanade.

For five years between 1873 and 1878 John Angel Gibbs and Company of Cardiff appeared in the Lloyds Register of Shipping as owner of the *John Peile*, 367 tons and 118 ft. long built in 1852 at Whitehaven and previously owned by his uncle, John Angel of Waterford, who was also her master until this change of ownership. During this time John Angel Gibbs was engaged in the Firm of Morel Brothers and Co. and his ownership of the *John Peile* must have been a marginal interest. He did not continue as an independent ship owner beyond this date, but identified himself completely with the Morel Firm.

Two matters from 1875 and 1876 have survived in the Firm's records: in

John Angel Gibbs and his wife Elizabeth in 1881 with their family — William (aged 7) Elizabeth (aged 5) John Angel (6 months) Susan (aged 3).

1875 James Strick & Sons who leased part of 2 Stuart Street gave up the lease before time: 'We are compelled to leave the premises immediately as we are unable to occupy them longer on account of bad smells there to which we have frequently directed your attention'. Morel Brothers were quite prepared to accept the surrender of the lease; they needed more room and they were preparing to rebuild their office building. And in February 1876 Morel Brothers receive the following letter written in H.G. Farrell's superb handwriting, which gives some indication of the conditions of work in a shipping office at that date:

'Cardiff, 10th February, 1876.
Messrs. Morel Brothers & Co.,
Cardiff.

Gentlemen,

As this day completes the third year of my engagement I have thought the present a fitting opportunity to lay before you a few small matters (or grievances) connected with the post which I have the honour to occupy in your office, viz: that of Confidential Clerk and bookkeeper and I assure you, gentlemen, I do so with the greatest reluctance and am only prompted to take this step by a feeling that the time has come when we should understand the exact relationship existing between us.

I would first call your attention to the arrangement entered into between your Mr. Philip Morel and myself in Jan 4/73 when I was informed that my duties (after the first six months) would not occupy more than five or six hours per day and upon those grounds I allowed the advance in my salary to be cut down ten pounds per annum.

Hitherto I have refrained from making any complaint owing to the several alterations and changes your staff have undergone during the short time I have been with you and the death of your esteemed brother and it being farthest from my thought to take the advantage of the position in which you were then placed. I feel sure you must be cognizant of the fact that my duties during the last 12 months have been heavy, which is easily accounted for seeing 21,500 tons of pitwood was invoiced in addition to usual office work including over 1000 vessels cleared and in order to meet which (and owing to the amount of juniors work imposed upon me) I have been obliged to work overtime to the extent of 622 hours, after allowing usual office hours and holidays. Now, gentlemen, I must ask you to take this matter into your serious consideration and upon no pretence allow my duties to be interrupted by the introduction of work altogether outside and foreign to my engagement and so give me an opportunity to acquit myself to your entire satisfaction without overtaxing and so prevent another illness which last year so marred my holiday and cost me a heavy doctors bill which I could ill afford out of so small a salary.

I much regret that on more than one occasion unkind remarks had been made respecting my leaving the office on Saturdays (which I have done on seven occasions only) earlier than on other days and I cannot conceive any reason why I am not to enjoy the recognized custom of early closing on that day in company with those in similar situations at the docks, seeing I take no dinner hour and as a rule am at my post an hour earlier than my neighbours and I trust you will throw no obstacle in the way of my leaving at three o'clock every Saturday for the future.

I will not add to the length of this letter by referring to the many circumstances which have occurred in the office during my term of service to cause my better feelings to recoil but beg to ask you to extend to me such general treatment as my position demands and give me information and assistance necessary for carrying on the work to the credit of the establishment and satisfaction of all parties.

Trusting the year just entered upon will prove a very prosperous one to the firm and a blessed and happy one to the individual partners and their families.

I am, Gentlemen,
your obedient servant
H.G. Farrell.'

No reply to this letter is in existence. As we shall see H.G. Farrell remained with the Firm for many years as 'confidential clerk and secretary'. It may be that the letter had its intended effect, although it is doubtful whether the hours were relaxed to any extent. A later manager of the Firm between 1925 and 1945 records that he, too, never got home before 6.00p.m. on Saturdays which was his only half day. Some twenty years later, in 1896, it is known that H.G. Farrell was reckoned to be 'an influential man with some property who has several good appointments as an accountant and auditor'.

From the 1870s onwards, the first steamships were beginning to appear in Cardiff Docks. From Thomas Morel's Obituary Notice;

> 'In the early 70's steam was just beginning to revolutionize shipping and, with that foresight and business acumen which always characterised him, Thomas Morel lost no time in adapting his business to modern requirements and the money made during the days of the sailing vessels was laid out in steamers.'

With the purchase in 1876 of the steamship, the *Colstrop*, built by Swans of Newcastle, Morel Brothers moved into the age of steam, being persuaded of the great advantages of steam power over sail: reliability and speed. Charter Parties could be entered into knowing that they could be fulfilled within the time agreed. There was not the need to wait for a wind or to sail where the winds were favourable. A steady average speed of 8 to 9 knots had been maintained by steamships built as early as the 1850s. The disadvantages were the costs; the initial cost of building iron ships and the cost of the fuel and the firemen's wages, which had to be added to the daily running expenses of each ship. By these, the Morels were not deterred.

They were by no means pioneers in this field, but once they had entered it they bent all their energies to building up a fleet of steamships under their own flag.

CHAPTER FOUR

The Move into Steam, 1876-1888

The Siren and Shipping, the periodical of the British Merchant Navy on 1st June, 1898 devoted its 'Headlight' to Thomas Morel. Included was the following paragraph.

> 'Messrs. Morel are however most widely known as steamship owners, and it is interesting to find that their first venture in this branch was made in 1876 when they acquired the "Colstrup". From then, for about ten years ship followed ship in quick succession — nearly all of them being specially constructed for the Bilbao iron ore trade, which the firm to a great extent made its own, although by no means neglecting other openings which presented themselves for the profitable employment of steam tonnage'.

The SS *Colstrup* of 319 net tons and an overall length of 159 ft. had been built by Swans of Newcastle in 1874. Her managing owner was John Mordecai Almond of Bute Docks, Cardiff, and in March 1876 she was in Dieppe, having been seized for non-payment of either crew's wages or ship's stores.

In the same month C.S. Swan, one of the founders of the Newcastle shipbuilding firm, later to be known as Swan Hunter, was visiting Cardiff and having met the Morel Brothers, he made a proposition to them that, if Thomas Morel would go to Dieppe and secure her release, he would arrange for the Morels to acquire shares in her. He gave Thomas Morel his power of attorney to negotiate on his behalf in France. C.S. Swan clearly believed that some one fluent in French could secure her release more effectively than he could.

In this Thomas succeeded and when debts on the steamer, both in France and in England, for which C.S. Swan acknowledged responsibility, were cleared, a number of transactions in the shares were recorded. Thomas Clarke and Co. of 4, Crockherbtown sold 4/64th as trustees to Morel Brothers for one hundred pounds, giving a value for the total vessel of £1,600. Twelve years later the ship was valued at between £3,100 and £4,500.

The next steamship to be bought was the SS *Portugalette* of 371 net tonage and overall length of 180.5 ft. built in 1877 by Palmers Ship Building and Iron Ore Company of Jarrow on Tyne. It would seem that the *Portugalette* was already laid down, perhaps even launched, when Morel Brothers and Company bought her. There are no specifications, contract note or correspondence in the Company records such as exist for other early Palmers ships. There are, however, two Bills of Sale extant. The first is a transfer to Philip Morel of nine sixtyfourth shares for £1,754. and the second is a transfer to Philip Le Moignan now living at Coin Varim, St. Peters, Jersey of three sixtyfourth shares for £500. On the assumption that the first transaction represents a proper proportion of the total price paid she would have cost about £12,500 and, presumably, because Philip Le Moignan started his nephews in business, the shares were sold to him at a discount of £28 per share.

Twenty-five ships followed in quick succession. In the year 1882, Morel Brothers took delivery of no fewer than nine new ships.

The naming of the early ships in the Morel Fleet reflected their trading areas and their family interests and connections. Welsh iron and steel towns intermingled with small towns in France and places in the Basque region of Spain; Portugalette is the harbour area of Bilbao, Galdames, the name given to the third ship, is a mountain nearby. Later, there is a reference to the island of origin of the Morels in the SS *Jersey* and a tribute to the Bute family in the SS *Ninian Stuart*. In 1899, they marked their involvement in the South American trade with the SS *Parana*, named after the river.

Morel Brothers and Company rebuilt 2 Stuart Street as offices from which to manage the rapidly growing fleet. The style was Venetian with rooms on the first floor with a fine view, not of a canal, but of the Bristol Channel.

The bills of exchange used by the Firm bore a facsimile of this building with passers-by on a reduced scale to increase its apparent size. The bills were still at this time printed in French with the claim 'Fondée 1865' which was after the date that Jean Morel began his chartering activities but was well before Philip and Thomas went ahead on their own in 1867.

There was ever increasing work; the ordering and management of new ships, ship broking and chartering of ships especially for the export of coal, the development of the trade with Bilbao, the importing of pit props, indeed, 'any openings which presented themselves for the profitable employment of steam tonnage'.

H.G. Farrell continued with the Company as confidential clerk. John Angel Gibbs was by now a full partner in the Firm with his Morel brothers-in-law and acting on behalf of the Company in the selling and buying of shares in the ships.

John Angel Gibbs's brothers, William Benjamin and Robert, increased the turnover of their ship-chandling business at the Pier Head. In 1894, after some thirty years trading, it was estimated that the senior partner, William Benjamin, had amassed a capital of £35,000 from the business.

The Gibbs family had a stronger connection with their island of origin, Portland, than had the Morels with Jersey. They maintained contact with their relatives and with their properties on the Island. John Angel Gibbs's marriage in the Fortuneswell Wesleyan Chapel in Portland to Elizabeth Pearce Scriven had been within the extended family as her middle name bore witness, his eldest sister, Sarah, having married a Pearce.

Elizabeth was a sweet, rather unintelligent girl who, throughout her life, let things happen to her rather than taking any hand in their direction. Even in her old age it was her daughters who decided that, being deaf, she must learn lip reading and then, when she was discovered in tears over the difficulties, that she must give it up without a proper trial. By contrast, John Angel had energy for concerns far beyond those of the Company; he 'was often called on to preside at meetings of a philanthropic character and he was appreciably regarded for integrity and geniality'. By 1880, when they moved to 17 St. Andrew's Crescent in the increasingly fashionable central area of Cardiff, he threw himself into the developing activities of the growing working class area of Cathays centred on the Wesleyan Chapel in Crwys Road. There, the minister, the young John Scott Lidgett, later to be a nationwide leader of Methodism and President of the Uniting Methodist Conference of 1932, was establishing a centre for religious life and social concern — to his thinking the two were of equal importance — and John Angel Gibbs became the Superintendent of the Sunday School, and also later Circuit Steward, the two most significant spheres of service for any layman within the Church.

In the words of the author of the Jubilee booklet of this Chapel he was 'a man of lovely character'.

As noted, Morel Brothers and Company decided by 1877 that the time had come to order ships on their own account and through the good offices of Mr. John Cory of John Cory and Sons, they approached Edward Holden, the London agent of Palmers Shipbuilding and Iron Ore Company of Jarrow. By 1876 John Cory and Sons owned three steamships and had already established a working relationship with Palmers for the building of ships specially designed for the iron ore trade with shallow draught to enable them to cross the bar at the entrance to the harbour at Bilbao. At first the Corys owned more steamships than the Morels. By 1882 each Company owned fourteen ships; after that date, the Morels went ahead and in 1886 owned twenty five steamers to the Corys' eighteen. They were rivals in the sense that both Companies were engaged in the iron ore trade, but whilst there remained ore to be mined in the mountains around Bilbao they did not need to compete for freights.

Both the Morels and the Corys claimed to have invented the flat-bottomed type of steamer to overcome the difficulty of navigating the Bilbao River. The obituary of Philip Morel as the partner most concerned with the designing and construction of the steamers, stated that 'this gave them a great advantage over other shipowners engaged in the Bilbao trade inasmuch as their vessels could cross the bar with full cargoes whilst others could only do so with half cargoes' — due to their depth of keel.

As both the Morels and the Corys were having ships built by Palmers Shipbuilding and Iron Company of Jarrow, from the late 1870s onwards, principally for the Spanish iron ore trade, it is likely that Palmers built a similar type of ship for both firms and that Palmers, as the shipbuilders, should properly be joined with them in the invention, which became standard practice as steamships surplanted sailing ships.

Edward Holden steered Morel Brothers and Company through their negotiations with Palmers. The Articles of Agreement for the laying down of a new ship, later to be known as the SS *Galdames*, were signed on 15th, May 1877. The iron two masted rigged schooner with two engines and an estimated speed of 8½ knots in ordinary weather was to cost £12,525 and to be ready for delivery on, or before, 18th January, 1878. The specification of the steamer was to be; length, 220 ft., breadth, 30 ft. and depth of hold, 15 ft. 6. The equipment was exhaustively listed down to 'one hencoop', 'three boat bailers', 'one cruet stand of good quality'.

Morel Brothers received a letter from Edward Holden at the same time as the copy of the Agreement which detailed the method of payment. When the vessel was 'framed' £1,550 was to be paid, £1,550 when the vessel was plated and a further sum of £3,162.10.0d. when it was delivered to the purchasers. These payments were to be made only against Lloyds Surveyor's certificates that the construction had advanced to the appropriate stage.

After delivery the builders retained a mortgage on the ship which was to be paid off against Bills of Exchange in five installments at regular intervals, starting six months after the delivery, until the full £12,525 was paid. Money towards this would begin to come in to the owners as soon as the ship was working and Edward Holden assured Morel Brothers that this would be at a rate of not less than £10 to £15 a day.

Morel Brothers were fearful of an insurance clause which assigned the policy to the builders 'on demand' if the vessel was lost during the currency of any of the Bills of Exchange. Privately, Edward Holden informed Morel Brothers that Palmers had included this clause to protect themselves from unprincipled people.

> '. . . the fact exists that one party who was owing a large sum of money on a Bill of Exchange for a boat as soon as the boat was lost drew the money from the underwriters, bolted and never paid the bill. However, you will see it is so worded "on demand" purposely you are not bound by contract to give up any policy unless asked for, which with respectable persons like yourselves — and Mr. Cory — is never done.'

Morel Brothers asked for a penalty clause of £3 a day for late delivery. Palmers bridled at this and Edward Holden wrote:

> 'First, Palmers and Co. simply object on a point of principle. They say "we agree to deliver a boat on a certain day and we mean to do so. The customers ask us to give credit on their promise to fulfil their engagement. We trust them. Surely they can trust us."'

The point was further made that the omission of such a clause was really in the buyers' interest:

> '. . . if the builders do not deliver you the boat on the day agreed then they have broken their contract — unless delay is due to fire, storm, tempest, strikes of workmen or other unavoidable circumstances — and the buyers have the power then to leave the damages which they incur to arbitration — and you may be quite sure they would be allowed pretty nearly what the boat would have earned — at least £10 to £15 per day.'

The boat was satisfactorily delivered and a relationship of mutual trust established which resulted in the ordering of a large number of ships from Palmers over the next decade.

Money for the purchase of this vessel would have come from the sale of shares in the vessel to shareholders. The Company itself would have been able to contribute a capital sum by ploughing into its new ship profits made in the management of its other ships and from the profits of its other activities such as chartering, and pit prop importing. The partners, using their growing personal fortunes, would take up shares in their own ships and from the dividends received capital could be invested in still more ships so that the Fleet could be increased, sometimes by as many as eight new ships in one year. In the case of the SS *Galdames*, the partners in Morel Brothers and Company took up a number of shares. On 11th June, 1878 the Company transferred ten of their sixty-four shares to Philip Morel for £2,500. Assuming that this represented ten sixty-fourths of the value of the ship it would seem that the partners in the Company considered that their entrepreneural activities in ordering and completing the purchase of the ship was worth in the region of £3,500. The ship cost the Firm £12,500 and the price received for the 64 shares was £16,000 if other buyers paid for their shares at the same rate as Philip Morel. This is borne out by a transaction recorded on the 17th of the same month in which Philip Morel sold one of his shares for £250 to Jacques Victor Valette of 52 Partridge Road, Cardiff. There was clearly a market for the shares in the new ship at this figure.

Morel Brothers followed the common practice of shipowners of forming a new company for each ship as a means of limiting the liability of the Company to the value of any one ship, if the ship was, indeed, lost.

When a new ship was building in 1881 — to be known later as the SS *Merthyr* — it was sold by Morel Brothers and Company to a company known as 'the Merthyr Steamship Company Limited,' in the case of this particular ship, for £24,000. The Agreement was couched in the following terms:

> 'The vendors or the survivors or survivor shall be the first Directors and Managers of the Company. After the death of the survivor, the Director and Manager shall be the person or persons who may from time to time be members of the firm of Morel Brothers and Company.
>
> The Directors shall perform all the usual duties of ship's husband and manager

IS Lesraulx, the first, built in 1880 by W. Doxford of Sunderland, in the Avon Gorge, Bristol.

IS Pontypridd, the first, built in 1883 by the Blythe Shipbuilding Company of Blythe, in the Avon Gorge, Bristol.

of the Company. They shall have power to purchase or contract for another steamship.

The remuneration of the Directors and Manager shall be three per cent on the gross earning of the steamship managed by them. The firm of Morel Brothers and Co. shall act as the shipbrokers of the Company and shall receive their usual and customary brokerage on the negotiations of charters or contracts in addition to the remuneration reserved to them as above.'

The advantage of such contracts to the Company was clear; the liability of Morel Brothers and Company was 'limited' — in so far as it related only to this one ship, and their remuneration was fixed at a considerable proportion of the gross earnings in addition to the normal brokerage profits.

This pattern of ownership, first documented in the papers of the SS *Merthyr*, which began trading in 1882, was the norm for ships owned by Morel Brothers and Company at this time. When shipping was profitable the return both to the individual shareholders in the ships and to the ships' managers was considerable.

When conditions made it possible for a company to trade profitably and they were competent enough to take advantage of these conditions, there was a regular income from the management and brokerage services and, in addition, a fluctuating return based on the gross earnings of the ships they managed. The purchasers of the shares showed by their investment a confidence in the management skills of a particular shipping company. They had expectations of a return on their capital which might, in a good year, be very high indeed. 'During the relatively brief stages of prosperity large profits are made on the average which enable shipping firms as a whole to cover the original cost of their investments and, at the same time, to compensate them for their long run costs in the lean years in which profits may not be made at all.'[1] Such periods of prosperity enabled the management to raise enough capital to order new ships and so increase the size of their fleet or replace old tonnage, or take their profit and use it elsewhere.

Records are extant for the shareholdings in, and the dividends paid in, the SS *Longueil* Steamship Co. from her building in 1882 until 1888, which reveal striking fluctuations in trading profits.

It will be noted that at this date, the division of ship holdings into 64 shares has given place to a division into 100 shares.

In the SS *Longueil* Steamship Company dividends were paid quarterly for 1882/1883.

Dividend per share paid in	July 1882	13.17.5
	November 1882	13.0.0.
	February 1883	9.1.11.
	May 1883	8.2.7.
Income from 12 months on one share		£44.1.11

Dividend Distribution on 100 shares		£4,409.11.8

for 1883/1884

Dividend per share paid in	July 1883	11.18.11
	November 1883	4.13.9
	March 1884	1.0.10
	June 1884	4.2.9
Income for 12 months on one share		£21.16.3
Dividend Distribution on 100 shares		£2,181.50

for 1884/1885

Dividend per share paid in	September 1884	nil
	December 1884	1.10.0
	February 1885	nil
	May 1885	nil
Income for 12 months on one share		£1.10.0
Dividend Distribution on 100 shares		£150

for 1885/1886

Dividend per share paid in	July 1885	nil
	November 1885	7.0.0.
	February 1886	nil
	May 1886	nil
Income for 12 months on one share		£7.0.0
Dividend distributed on 100 shares		£700.0.0d.

for 1886/1887

Dividend per share paid in	July 1886	nil
	November 1886	nil
	February 1887	nil
	May 1887	nil
Income for 12 months on one share		nil
Dividend distributed on 100 shares		nil

for 1887/1888

Dividend per share paid in	July 1887	nil
	October 1887	8.0.0.
	February 1888	10.0.0.

Income for three quarters of a year on one share £18.0.0d.
Dividend distributed on three quarters of a year on 100 shares £1,800.0.0d.

There was clearly a serious slump in the type of shipping in which Morels were engaged between 1885 and 1887. By 1888 the slump was ending, enabling a substantial dividend to be paid on 1st February, 1888 following on the previous good dividend in October 1887. In 1888 freight rates were abnormally high. The figures indicate very clearly the considerable fluctuations in dividends over this period of six years; the traditional 'good and bad years'. They do not, however, indicate the actual financial returns to Morel Brothers and Company. By receiving brokerage on the charters they negotiated — the ships will normally have continued to trade even during the bad years — and the 3% on the gross profit, which will have been considerable between 1882 and 1884, they will at least have earned enough to remain in business until the peak year of 1888, which will have brought a considerable addition to their capital assets.

The shareholdings in the SS *Longueil* held by any one person were small. Out of the 100 shares, 64 persons held one share, 11 persons two shares, 2 persons held three shares and 2 persons four shares.

The geographical distribution of the holdings of these one hundred shares can be categorised as follows:

Cardiff and Penarth	25 shares
South Wales (other than Cardiff or Penarth)	16 shares
England	2 shares
Jersey	6 shares
France	49 shares
Belgium	2 shares

Of the immediate family, Philip and Thomas Morel held one share each and John Angel Gibbs and William Benjamin Gibbs one share each: For the first year Morel Brothers and Company held two shares which they sold in the subsequent year. There were no women owners amongst the British names — the Married Women's Property Act of 1884 had not yet come into effect — but on Jersey and in France there were eight madames and one mademoiselle.

The French and Belgian shareholders, which it will be noted form the larger group, were clustered mainly around La Rochelle, Poitiers and Tonnay Charente. There were two distinguished names: M. le Marquis Ernest de Villedon, au Chateau Inferieur de Montagne par la Jarrie, and Mr. le Commandant de St. Martin La Coutaire, part L'Isle en Dodon, Haute Garonne.

This large continental holding — over 50% of the shareholding and built up, presumably, from trading contacts in France — was to have a dramatic influence in the year 1884.

In 1884, Morel Brothers and Company were at a high point of activity. The East Dock in Cardiff known sometimes, apparently, as 'Morel Dock', might at any one time be full with up to thirty ships chartered by Morels and loading coal. The fleet of ships that they had built or bought comprised some twenty-six vessels, the older ones comparatively small, but some fine new larger ships with the SS *Ninian Stuart* the pride of the fleet. The iron ore trade with Bilbao was to a considerable extent in their hands. From a position where they sold shares in their ships to anyone who would buy, they now began to pursue a policy of the Company itself taking up all the shares and paying for the complete ship out of the very considerable resources at its disposal.

To control all these activities Philip and Thomas Morel and John Angel Gibbs, working in partnership, had a staff of fifteen at 2 Stuart Street: Confidential Clerk — Mr. H.G. Farrell, Bookkeeper — Mr. Rutter, Cashier — Mr. Charles Isdebski, Correspondent — Mr. Hood. Accounts Department — Messrs. Broomfield, Trice, Morel (John), Sandy and Hooper. Chartering Department — Messrs. Walsh, William, Martin, Morgan, Hamon and Sweeney.

On Friday, 4th April, 1884 John Angel Gibbs, aged 35, caught a chill and died of pneumonia and pleurisy on Good Friday a week later. He left a widow and five children and a sixth to be born posthumously. The Wesleyan Methodist Church mourned him the next Sunday by draping in black all the pulpits in the Cardiff Circuit. At the funeral service, attended by shipowners from the North of England, London and seaports in South Wales, John Scott Lidgett gave the address and the pall bearers were John Angel Gibbs's fellow stewards. The press noted that 'At the conclusion of the mournful ceremony a large number of Sunday School children descended the vault steps and deposited wreathes and bunches of flowers upon the coffin until it was hidden by floral beauty.'

On 16th April the captains of twenty six ships drew up an illuminated memorial address:

> 'We, the undersigned Master Mariners in the employ of Messrs. Morel Brothers and Company, wish to express to Mrs. Gibbs and her children our earnest and heartfelt sympathy on the terrible bereavement they have sustained in the sudden and painful death of a beloved husband and father, the late Mr. John Angel Gibbs, who was one of the Founders of the largest Fleet of Steamships belonging to the Port of Cardiff.
>
> We also desire to place on record our deep sense of the many acts of kindness shown to us individually during the time we have been in his employ; his untiring zeal and energy at all times displayed in promoting our highest and best interests call for the warmest gratitude and admiration of us all.'

John Angel Gibbs's death made necessary a valuation of the holdings of the partners in Morel and Company. Two valuations of the fleet were obtained and the figures varied in some particulars as a number of the vessels were not available for inspection. The two valuations are included in Appendix Two with the proportion of the shares held bv Morel Brothers and Company themselves in each vessel. The policy of the Company of owning all the shares in a ship had been implemented in the case of the SS *Penarth*, the SS *Allende* and the SS *Ninian Stuart*.

The total value of the ninety two shares in the 23 steamers held by the Company was £18,460.7.0d. and the value of the shares held in the three wholly owned ships amounted to £79,185.15.5d.

John Angel Gibbs's will was proved for £21,732. His estate, apart from small holdings in individual ships, which were retained for the immediate present, and small holdings in the Cardiff Junction Dry Dock and Engineering Company and the Bute Shipbuilding, Engineering and Dry Dock Company, with two life insurance policies and his house in Andrews Crescent, was comprised entirely of his third share of Morel Brothers and Company. This probate figure was considerably less than the £32,545 to which his estate should have been entitled at the very least on the basis of his ownership of a third of the Companies' assets. It would be customary to write the estate down to its lowest possible figure and, indeed, as the Company was a private one there was no guarantee that on a hypothetical sale of the assets — the shares in the ships — they would be able to be realized for their estimated value. In addition to a claim on the shares of the Company there would also be a figure for the partnership rights which would have been considerable, howbeit difficult to assess.

Whatever the figure at which probate for the estate was granted, it was beholden upon the executors, John Angel Gibbs's two brothers, William Benjamin and Robert, to press for payment at the figure indicated by the valuation, with a sum in addition for the partnership rights.

The consequences upon Morel Brothers of John Angel Gibbs's death were traumatic. The loss of an able and energetic member of the partnership was indicated to correspondents by the heavy black edges to the writing paper which the Company adopted, but this did not reveal the financial crisis in the Firm at a time when shipping was at a low ebb as revealed by the figures for the Longueil Steamship Company for 1885 and the two subsequent years.

As if these difficulties were not enough, what the partners described as the Vero affair required their immediate attention. The large French shareholding in the individual ship companies was normally quiescent but at this precise moment the financial difficulties of two of the French shareholders had repercussions on the Firm and also on the relationship between the Morels and the Gibbs.

In October 1882, Thomas Morel had been in negotiation with a M. A. Vero of La Rochelle about the taking up of shares in ships then being built. Thomas Morel suggested that payment for these shares should be on the same terms as those granted to a relative of M. Vero's, a M. Millonair:

> 'To do this without displacing your funds we should recommend you to place part

of them, say half, and hold the remainder; you can easily do this in France and England as our shares are more and more sought after and are at a premium.'

M. Vero took up shares in the SS. *Longueil*, but neither he, nor M. Millonair had paid in full for their shares in the various Morel ships as late as two years after taking them up and in May 1884 Morel Brothers and Company pressed them for payment. M. Vero was advised by a firm of London solicitors, Ashurst, Morris, Crisp and Co. of 6 Old Jewry E.C. The solicitors counter-claimed by requiring that their client's name be removed from the register of three of the Steamship Companies, thus indicating that they refused to admit that M. Vero had ever taken up shares in the Companies. They further requested information about what had taken place at the last General Meeting 'failing the receipt of which they would take legal proceedings to enforce the shareholders' rights'.

The matter was further exacerbated by the financial difficulties of Vero's relative, M. Millonair, who apparently was unable to pay but who, Thomas Morel hoped, would be bailed out by his son-in-law Alfred Renaud — whom Thomas seemed to know and whom he considered to be 'at the bottom of all this'.

Within a month of John Angel Gibbs's death, Philip had to go to Paris to negotiate payment for the shares and Thomas briefed him as to the line he should take. If the two French shareholders, having received dividends on the shares, continued to refuse to pay for them 'it would mean a loss to the Firm of £5,000 to £6,000. We ought to push these people and obtain a settlement of the whole question'. Thomas estimated that if they had to take back the shares at the time of writing they were 'not worth half the amount they represent — consequently we must treat them as worth 50% or less'.

This situation, not uncommon in the life of an expanding company, was further complicated by the threat that John Angel Gibbs's death posed to the financial stability of the Company. Philip and Thomas were faced with the need to find a very large sum of money. Yet, to pay over one third of the assets of the Company to William Benjamin and Robert Gibbs as executors of their brother's estate at the crucial stage of the Company's development, when its assets were basically confined to holdings in the various steamship companies, would strain their resources almost to breaking point. William Benjamin and Robert, aware that their sister-in-law, Elizabeth, would need a secure income to support herself and her six children, very properly, expected payment in full of their brother's share in Morel Brothers and Company so that they could reinvest it in gilt-edged Trustee stock.

Philip and Thomas were driven to explore ways by which the executors could be persuaded not to require the realization of the assets of the Firm. They even explored the possibility of William Benjamin taking over his late brother's place in Morel Brothers and Company.

They put the suggestion to their solicitors, Ingledew, Ince and Vachell of Cardiff that William Benjamin Gibbs should be appointed to the management of the Beignon and Longueil Steamship Companies — and presumably of the other Companies — so as to share in the remuneration for the management of the vessels. Somewhat ingenuously, they proposed that this should be effected by putting the matter to a vote of the shareholders of the companies, thinking that they would be able to secure a majority at a meeting called for the purpose of ratifying William Benjamin Gibbs's appointment, 'as the French shareholders would not attend personally'.

The solicitors, however, thought otherwise; they pointed out that M. Vero was at present being advised by London solicitors and that when M. Vero informed his solicitors that there was to be a proposal to appoint a third Manager and Director, they would advise the French shareholders to attend the meeting and vote directly, or by proxy, against the motion. The French and Belgian shareholders held over 50% of the shares in the Longueil Company and could defeat the proposal.

Ingledew, Ince and Vachell further pointed out that by the Articles of the Company, which were identical with those of the SS *Merthyr*, Thomas and Philip Morel and John Angel Gibbs were appointed jointly and separately Managers and Directors and, as another Article provided that the Managers and Directors might consist of only two members, there were no grounds for increasing the number of the Managers. Indeed, they suggested firmly that it was impossible to do so within the Articles of the Company. Philip and Thomas Morel must continue to act on their own and perform all the duties of the Managers of the Company.

The proposal that William Benjamin Gibbs should take his brother's place by this procedure was clearly improper. Presumably William Benjamin had been consulted as to the possibility of this and had agreed to it being considered. As senior Executor two possible courses of action had been open to him; either to leave his brother's estate in Morel Brothers and Company and watch over its interests to the best of his ability, or to require that it be paid out in cash which could then be reinvested. If he were to take his late brother's place in the Company this would have enabled him to watch over the estate's interests at first hand and would also be to his considerable financial advantage. This latter aspect of the matter cannot be ignored. Put crudely, the scheme was an attempt to influence William Benjamin Gibbs to leave the assets of the Estate with the Company. At that stage it was impossible for William Benjamin to tell whether or not this would be to the advantage of his late brother's family. The proposal proved, however, not to be possible, at least in the form put up to the solicitors by Morel Brothers, and William Benjamin, with his fellow Executor Robert, was left to take the latter course. This required that a third of the assets of Morel Brothers and Company be realized and paid over so that they could be invested in Trustee Stock.

For a short period it seemed that William Benjamin Gibbs might have become as prominent a Cardiff docksman as his brother and brothers-in-law. He was one of the original directors of the Bute Shipbuilding, Engineering and Dry Dock Company, presumably in his brother's place. William Benjamin Gibbs, however, was not to follow his brother into the shipowning world with its risks and its heady profits, nor was he to follow him for any length of time as superintendent of the Cathays Wesleyan Sunday School, although he served as such temporarily. He was a different man from his brother and it was unrealistic to expect him to take over his brother's place and responsibilities because of that brother's death in middle age. He remained a substantial ship-chandler and maintained strongly his interests and connection with the Isle of Portland. Later he was to move to Weston-super-Mare where he could live his own life away from the somewhat overpowering Morel influences.

Thomas and Philip Morel were in a grave position. They had few resources other than those tied up in the Company and in the ships. They managed, however, to find the sum that the Executors agreed represented John Angel Gibbs's interest in Morel Brothers. The Lloyds list of 1890-1 showed that the SS *Allende* and the SS *Penarth* were no longer listed as the property of Morel Brothers and Company but appeared under the Forest Steamship Co. Ltd. and the Treherbert Steamship Co. Ltd. Both ships continued to be managed by Morel Brothers and Company but were no longer in their ownership, the shares in them having been sold to raise the capital required. By this means and by other such steps they found the money needed to meet John Angel Gibbs's share in the Company — but they nearly became bankrupt in the process. The Firm weathered the storm but the repercussions of the withdrawal of capital affected relations between the two families for 75 years, and even between the two branches of the Gibbs family. The Morels always felt that they had advanced John Angel Gibbs to the position of partner and that he should never have died when he did. In effect, his services were withdrawn and a very considerable part of the assets from the Firm were withdrawn as a result, at a critical stage in its development nearly bringing about its destruction. They were unprepared thereafter to consider anyone of that name as a partner in the Firm.

The children of John Angel Gibbs came to regret the action of their uncles, the two Executors. They watched the firm of Morel Brothers prosper, and projected how their father's share, if it had not been withdrawn, would have increased proportionately. They were aware of the contrast in their fortunes, locked primarily in Trustee Stock, with those of their cousins. They always retained a resentment against their uncles, William Benjamin and Robert, for the action which they had taken with complete propriety but with such unforeseen and unforeseeable consequences.

Of the outcome of the Vero affair there is no record; its significance was not in itself but that it exacerbated the difficulties caused by the death of John Angel Gibbs and further strained the relationships between the Morel brothers and William Benjamin Gibbs on the death of his brother.

Morel Brothers and Company continued with their many-sided activities during this period. Their most important importing trade was that of the iron ore from Bilbao in which both Morel Brothers and John Cory & Sons continued to claim the distinction of leading the field. Between 1880 and 1888 there are twenty seven letters in the Dowlais Iron Company records from Morel Brothers and Company all dealing with the supply of Iron Ore to the works for their steel making processes. On 9th September, 1880 Morel Brothers offered 10,000 tons of Companil ore to be delivered between September and June. The Dowlais Company offered 16/3 per ton but Morels pointed out that they were asked 9/6 per ton at Bilbao and that freight at 8/6 would put the price at 18/ – ; however, they were prepared to accept 17/ – 'for a few cargoes'. In 1881, they quoted 16/ – per ton ex ship Cardiff between January and July. They underlined that they were able to offer these terms as they had special arrangements whereby waggons were sent to their wharf, 'at which they could obtain extra dispatch for their steamers'. In April 1881, 'one of our Firm is in Spain;' as the letter was in Philip's handwriting it would have been Thomas. They offered to secure 10,000 to 15,000 tons of Companil ore over the next six months at 13/6 per ton ex ship at Cardiff. Later in the month Philip wrote that 'we should not make the delivery of 400 tons per day an obstacle to business.'

On occasion, Morel Brothers miscalculated. In September 1881 Thomas wrote to the Dowlais Iron Company: 'We shall be glad to make a compact with you for Companil and Rubio ore to run in conjunction with our present contract at the current rate which as you are aware is 15/ – per ton. The reason why we ask you to let us run this contract conjointly with the present one is that we make a heavy loss on the present one and it will enable us to recoup ourselves a trifle. Respecting the last contract although we partly covered ourselves in Spain, still, over the balance, there stands a margin of 1/6 per ton against us. The Rubio ore is of extra good quality containing 51% of iron ore, if you look at the results obtained from your furnaces, make yourselves sure that what we say is correct.'

By 1887, the price had fallen. During the summer months, Morel Brothers offered 'a quantity of Bilbao ore at 11/ – per ton guaranteed 50% in the raw, with a 4d. scale up or down'. Time and time again in their correspondence they made the point that with respect to their offers, 'it is only our position as shipowners enables us to do this'.

Two contracts are extant, which show that they both shipped coal as exporters and bought coal for shipment and resale abroad.

On 26th June, 1876 Morel Brothers were engaged to provide vessels to be loaded in Bute East, or Bute West Dock, or Penarth Dock to convey 6,000 tons to both Honfleur and Granville and 4,000 tons to Cherbourg and Brest. The freight was fixed for Honfleur at 11 francs 50 centimes per ton and at 10 francs for the other ports, a gratuity of 15 centimes per ton being paid to the captain of each vessel. The contract was for the year with discharge at the ports of 30 tons per day.

On 7th November of the same year Morel Brothers agreed to buy from the Powell Duffryn Steam Coal Co. ten thousand tons of steam coal — 'layer coal' to be shipped during the ensuing twelve months from Cardiff, Newport and Swansea. The price was 10/6 per ton less discount of 2½% for cash.

Morel Brothers and Company also bought pitwood from their French connections. On 6th July, 1877 George Aspells sold them 4,000 pit props of marketable lengths and fixed delivery about 1,000 tons per month from this date price 21/ – per ton ex ship at Cardiff, Newport or Swansea at the option of Morel Brothers.

On a less exacting level, as the brothers spoke both English and French fluently, they were called upon to act officially as interpreters. In June 1880, in a case heard before the Notary Public in Cardiff a sea captain protested that his late delivery of a cargo of pitwood was due to a sudden squall which almost drove his vessel on to the Vielle Rock, and Philip Morel translated the technical terms from French to English.

In addition to shipowning and chartering, however, the most remarkable activity of the Company was their venture into both ship repairing and ship building, the subject matter of the next chapter.

A quotation from Thomas Morel's obituary, although written in 1903 describes the situation in the period under review.

> 'As time went on steamers of larger tonnage were built, and entered into competition with those of other firms for the general trade of this country until at the present time Morel Ltd. owns a fleet of 32 steamers. Placed end to end they would extend considerably over a mile and it may be safely said that the Firm may be regarded as among the foremost shipowners in the British Channel if not in the country.
>
> The introduction of steam changed the whole aspect of the coal trade. Instead of that commodity being carried on vessels owned in foreign ports, the steamers engaged in the trade were built in England principally at Newcastle, but registered and managed at Cardiff, although many gentlemen of wealth in France, Spain and other countries took shares in them. The immediate effect was that crews were shipped at Cardiff instead of being shipped abroad and their families lived at Cardiff.'

The varying activities of the Morel Firm had become clearly related to the development of Cardiff and the growth of the Firm reflected in a not inconsiderable manner the growth of Cardiff itself.

CHAPTER FIVE

Morels as Shipbuilders

The Morel Brothers with six others, Lewis Williams, William Benjamin Gibbs, John Henry Murrel of West Hartlepool, George Renwick of Newcastle, Thomas Callaghan and David Duncan, acquired, in 1882, the shipbuilding yard which had been built by Messrs. Maudsley early in the 1860s. This was the Bute Ironworks Company of West Canal Wharf and early in 1883, under their manager, H.W. Lewis, they were trading under the comprehensive title of the Bute Shipbuilding, Engineering and Dry Dock Co. In August, the Marchioness of Bute laid the foundation stone of the Bute Graving Dock and in the same year the Company was incorporated with a capital of £175,000 of which £40 per share had been called and paid.

In 1885, they issued a prospectus inviting the public to subscribe for £60,000 mortgage debentures bearing interest at 5%. This described the properties on which the debentures would have the first charge:

> 'Firstly, the Bute Shipbuilding, Engineering and Foundry Works, advantageously situated on the River Taff, at Cardiff, connected by direct sidings with the Great Western Railway, with a river frontage of more than 500 feet, and covering an area of nearly four acres. These works have recently been put into thorough repair, extended and fitted with all the modern machinery and appliances necessary for carrying on shipbuilding, repairing, engineering and foundry work on an extensive scale, with economy of labour and dispatch. The machinery includes a large steam locomotive crane, and steam hammers, one of which has been specially erected for heavy forgings, thus rendering the works second to none in the neighbourhood, and supplying a long-felt necessity in Cardiff. A Jetty has been erected on the river, alongside which steamers of any tonnage can lie with safety to receive repairs to Hull or Machinery, and powerful Shear Legs and Appliances can be erected on the Jetty to enable ships' boilers, etc., to be removed. On the slipways several ships up to 400 ft. in length, can be constructed at one and the same time. The engine department has been specially arranged for the construction of engines of every description, and experience has proved that this is one of the greatest sources of profit in connection with steamship work. By the lease special power is given the lessees to construct slips for ship repairing; and with the present rapidly increasing trade at Cardiff, it will, probably, be in the interest of the Company to avail themselves of this privilege at an early date.
>
> Secondly, the Bute Dry Dock and Adjacent Engineering Works, at the South East end of the Roath Basin, covering an area of upwards of two-and-a half acres. This Dry Dock and Works, together with the machinery, offices, buildings, etc., have been constructed for carrying on a ship and engine repairing business on a large scale. The Dock, which is 600 feet long and 87 feet wide is specially designed to accommodate the largest class of vessels afloat, or four steamers of large tonnage at the same time. By means of caisson arrangements part of the Dock can be divided off in three places, and ships are enabled to continue their repairs dry whilst others are floated in and out. By a system of culverts connected with the

tideway the water is discharged from either end of the Dock without pumping. Arrangements have been made with the Marquis of Bute for the gates and capstans of the Company being connected with the hydraulic machinery which works the Bute Docks. By this means a great saving of time and labour in docking and undocking ships is effected. The direct access which is established between the Company's Dry Dock and the existing Roath Basin affords a direct communication with the Bute East Dock and also with the large New (Roath) Dock which the Marquis of Bute is now engaged in constructing: thus enabling the whole of the shipping frequenting that Basin and Docks to have Dry Dock accommodation always available, and it has been proved that the proximity of the Company's Dry Dock to those large undertakings, and the facilities which exist for ships being docked and undocked without risk, at any hour of the day or night, irrespective of tide, renders this property the most attractive of its kind in Cardiff.

Thirdly, the Treherbert Foundry and Engineering Works, comprising an area of about an acre, admirably situated on the Rhondda Branch of the Taff Vale Railway in the immediate neighbourhood of several large collieries. These works have been successfully carried on for several years past by Mr. H.W. Lewis, and include well arranged plant and machinery for the manufacture of all colliery engineering requirements and possessing special appliances for heavy castings.'

In the summer of 1885 H.W. Lewis, writing from the 'Shipbuilding Yard, Glamorganshire Canal', sought an interview with the Dowlais Iron Company and placed an order for 'a large quantity of girder plates'. He had previously written in July 1884, 'we are sorry you cannot supply the steel plates; we are introducing steel plates when iron was used before at the request of your general manager'.

In May 1886 the 'special commissioner' of the *South Wales Daily News* wrote a promotional 'inspired' article following on the launching of the SS *Collivaud* built for Morel Brothers and Company; a 'fine new steamer built entirely of steel'.

He firstly described the ship repairing facilities:

'. . . as I stood in the comfortable office tenanted by Mr. H.G. Farrell, the courteous and affable secretary to the Company, I could not help being strongly impressed by the admirable facilities for obtaining and executing orders of any magnitude at the disposal of that portion of the vast concern known as the Bute Dry Dock.

The extensive view obtained from the office window afforded a typical illustration of our maritime supremacy as a nation which was striking in the extreme. In the immediate foreground is the Roath Basin out of which extends the new Roath Dock, whilst away to the left the Bute East Dock curves into the dim distance until its outline is merged in a forest of masts, rendered still more indistinct by the clouds of smoke curling upwards from the funnels of apparently countless steamers.

Behind this picture of commercial life and activity lies a misty panorama of Cardiff veiled however in the present instance from ordinary observation by a slight drizzling rain.'

Then he described the history of the shipbuilding enterprise:

> 'The shipbuilding yard, situated on the river Taff was originally projected by Messrs. Scott Russell and Co., the eminent engineers, about seventeen years ago. The premises afterwards passed into the hands of Maudsley Brothers who were again succeeded by the well-known Shipowners, Morel Brothers. A spacious foundry and engineering works situated at Treherbert together with the Bute Dry Dock and adjacent works (then in the course of construction) were all the property of the firm but in 1883 they decided to transfer their sole interest to a limited company. A share list was issued, the bulk of the shares remaining in the hands of the vendors and the subscribed capital amounted to £175,000. Since that date everything has progressed smoothly and evenly and it speaks well for the managerial ability displayed by the Company that even in the present depressed state of trade generally they have managed to obtain constant and remunerative contacts.'

There then followed a somewhat surprising attack on the Marquis of Bute — considering how dependant Morel Brothers & Company were on the Bute Docks. However, the *South Wales Daily News* was a liberal paper with a deep-seated antipathy to the Castle and everything that proceeded from the Bute Estate Office.

> 'The single element of unpleasantness in this so far, prosperous and thriving record is the heavy ground rent demanded by the Marquis of Bute for the privilege of building splendid works upon what was previously a desert waste of stones and mud. This combined with the wretched leases granted to all who require them being limited to such a short period as 88 years under the most restricted and arbitrary conditions constitutes a genuine grievance felt by all trades alike in Cardiff and one which has done much towards driving away lucretive industries to other more favourable situations. This anomaly is rendered, in the present instance, more glaring from the fact that on the other side of the river a similar company has obtained a 250 years lease for double the area at one quarter of the cost. Here, however, the lord of the Manor was Lord Windsor.'

The 'commissioner' then walked around both the dry dock and the ship-building dock accompanied by Mr. Farrell, 'who proved to be a remarkably well informed guide.'

> 'I first visited the neighbouring Dry Dock which, even to the unscientific observer presented an appearance of vast dimensions and great resource. A continuous clang of heavy hammers wielded by the workmen resounded from the sides of the vessels undergoing repairs, proving most indubidably that Vulcan is still represented by worthy descendants.
>
> The majestic dock is easily capable of holding four large vessels at the same time and on one occasion recently there were 7,000 tons of shipping collected within its precints.
>
> The Bute Shipbuilding Engineering and Foundry Docks are situated on the river Taff and may be reached in a quarter of an hour's walk from the Dock . . . They may be regarded as second to no other — not even the old-established firms of the North East Coast. Taking into consideration the close proximity of iron and steel works together with the obvious advantage of being favourably situated in a

A general view of the Bute Shipbuilding, Engineering and Dry Dock Company. 1884.

The Bute Shipbuilding, Engineering and Dry Dock Company with a ship on the stocks. 1884.

town like Cardiff, there cannot fail to be a future of great scope before this department of the industry.

Before leaving this section I asked Mr. Farrell how much per ton a shipbuilding firm could turn out a vessel for now-a-days. "Well", he replied, "bearing in mind that the present price of steel plates averages about £6.10.0d. per ton and the distance from, say, Landore to Cardiff being trivial would render the railway charges comparatively slight, I should say that from £8 to £9 would be a remunerative figure for the builder and would not press heavily upon the purchase." How the shareholders in certain firms I know of in the North of England would groan at this when but two years ago they were paying £14 to £15 for the same class of vessel.

This Company occupies a very prominent position in the role of our Cardiff industries. It is equally well served by sea and land. The Bute Railway circumvents the dry dock on all sides and the Great Western runs into the shipbuilding yard. Presuming that they were all working full time, the yard would provide work for 1,200 men.'

The Lloyds Register of Shipping lists the three ships built during the 1880s, by the Bute Shipbuilding, Engineering and Dry Dock Company with Thomas Dobson as construction manager. The SS *Collivaud* built in 1886 for Morel Brothers and Co., which replaced an earlier SS *Collivaud* built in 1882. The SS *Cardiff Castle* built in 1889 for Morel Ltd., launched 26th October, and the SS *Mayfield* built in 1890 for Frederick Woods of 44 Leadenhall Street, London, and launched on 19th April, 1890.

1889 was to be the high point of shipbuilding in Cardiff; the high hopes of those engaged in the industry for a new Middlesborough or Jarrow were never fulfilled. The special commissioner who, after being shown around the Bute yard, predicted 'there cannot fail to be a future of great scope before this department of the industry' can be dismissed as partial but there were other no less enthusiastic voices. C. Watkins writing in 1903 noted 'When the need to import ores led the Merthyr Ironmasters to build a new plant at Cardiff in the 1880s it was expected that the town could become a shipbuilding centre'. At a considerably later date, Lloyd George, speaking to the Cardiff Chamber of Commerce in 1907, asked "Why should not South Wales and Cardiff develop into one of the greatest manufacturing centres in the whole Empire?".

It was on the success or failure of the Bute shipbuilding enterprise that the future of Cardiff as a centre for shipbuilding depended and Thomas Morel was prepared to put his energies into the Firm: 'I have always been willing to find capital and to give my time to pushing forward the development of ship building in Cardiff.' The story of what happened can be pieced together from the letters written by Thomas Morel to the Dowlais Iron Company, and the *Western Mail* reports of the launchings of the two ships, the *Cardiff Castle* in 1889 and the *Mayfield* in 1890.

Following the launching of the *Collivaud*, Morel Brothers placed orders for three ships, one in Cardiff with their own Bute Shipbuilding, Engineering and

Dry Dock Company, which would become No. 8 on their order book and the *Cardiff Castle* on her launching in 1889, and two in the North of England, one with Palmers of Jarrow and one with Pickersgill of Newcastle. Messrs. Palmers and Messrs. Pickersgill delivered their ships in 1888.

After some correspondence, which is not preserved, Thomas Morel had written on 6th December, 1887 to E.D. Martin of the Dowlais Iron Works, Dowlais:

> 'Personally, I am much vexed that my Firm has not been able to give their recent orders to build a steamer to the local builders at Cardiff, one of the principal obstacles being the impossibility of obtaining the plates at a corresponding rate to what they are obtainable at in the North. I am still very anxious that Cardiff should secure some of the orders that are being given. Another order for twelve hundred tons is being planned by a firm of local shipowners this week. The order is again falling to the North, although Cardiff shipowners would be only too glad to see ships built under their eyes. I should be glad if when you are next in Cardiff you would give me a few minutes interview.'

E.D. Martin must have met Thomas Morel and indicated both by word of mouth and in writing that he could only make plates available at one and the same price either for ship repairing or for ship building.

Thomas Morel wrote again on 12th January, 1888:

> 'There is a great difference between quoting for the price of a new ship than for repairs to a ship. In the latter case, it is easy to pay the current price. We shall be glad if you will reconsider your decision and name us your very lowest price for the quantity named in our last letter.'

In August, 1888 Thomas Morel wrote to Messrs. Guest, the London House of the Dowlais Company to engage their interest asking:

> ' if you can deliver 800 to 1000 tons of steel plates say between this and March and April next. This is another attempt to bring shipbuilding to Cardiff and we trust you will be able to give us a special quotation.'

The London House refused to be committed and passed the enquiry back to Dowlais. Thomas Morel wrote again:

> 'Cardiff, August 31 '88.
>
> to E.H. Martin, Esq.
>
> Dear Sir,
>
> I have a letter from Messrs. Guest and Co. to say that they are communicating with you re the enquiry we made.
>
> I personally trust you will endeavour to make a suitable offer. I do not ask you to do what your predecessor did to give the steel away to make a commencement but what I should like you to do would be to make such a low offer that would enable the Bute Shipbuilding Company to undertake the building of a boat or two and I foresee that if this is done several orders will follow which would continue largely to benefit the Dowlais Iron Co.
>
> For your guidance there are 12 steamers building for Cardiff owners of large size

which will represent about 14,000 tons of steel. There is no reason why the whole of these should not have been ordered from Cardiff.

Yours very truly,
Thomas Morel.'

There now follows a gap in the correspondence of a year and a quarter.

In the meantime the *Cardiff Castle* was launched and Thomas Morel and all associated with the launching spoke in heady terms of the prospects for shipbuilding in Cardiff. The *Western Mail* of 28th October, 1889 carried a full account of the launching.

'The largest ship ever built at Cardiff was successfully launched on Saturday morning from the Bute Shipbuilding, Engineering and Dry Dock Co. Works on the east bank of the river Taff. Although the hour fixed for the ceremony was 7.30a.m. a large crowd had assembled by that time, amongst those present being many of the principal shipowners and brokers at the Docks. It was intended that the ship, which had been named the *Cardiff Castle*, should be christened by Lady Bute on the occasion of her visit to Cardiff in August to present the new colours to the third battalion Welch Regiment but through unforseen circumstances the ceremony had to be postponed and it was performed on Saturday by Lady Lewis, who was accompanied by Sir William Thomas Lewis.

A platform had been erected at the bows of the vessel upon which a select company assembled. The bottle of champagne with which the vessel was christened was decorated with the Royal Stuart tartan and was suspended from the bows by a ribbon of red, white and blue. Punctually at 7.30 the ship, on board of which there were several persons, was liberated from the stocks and Lady Lewis having broken on her starboard bow the bottle of wine, she gracefully glided into the Taff amid ringing cheers. The ribbon by which the bottle was suspended was presented to Lady Lewis as a momento of the occasion. Miss Morel of Lavernock presented her ladyship with a very handsome bouquet ....

.... After the launch the invited guests sat down to an excellent breakfast laid by Mr. R.P. Culley of the Exchange Restaurent at the Offices of the Bute Shipbuilding Company. About 180, including 58 ladies, partook of the acceptable repast provided. Captain Pomeroy, the Dockmaster, proposed success to the *Cardiff Castle* and to Messrs. Morel Brothers, the owners. He was sure that they all felt proud of the successful launch on the banks of the Taff that morning of the fine vessel, the *Cardiff Castle* (applause). He would like to see a similar ceremony weekly, but perhaps that would be too much to expect, but they might have one monthly. Messrs. Morel Bros. had been very fortunate in building the *Cardiff Castle* when they did as they would not be able to lay her down for anything like the same money in the future. He hoped that the *Cardiff Castle* would have good freights and plenty of them (Applause).

Mr. Thomas Morel in acknowledging the toast took advantage of that opportunity to publicly thank Sir W.T. Lewis and Lady Lewis for having come down to the yard at so early an hour to take part in the ceremony. He (Mr. Morel) has taken a great interest in the question of shipbuilding at Cardiff (Applause). Capt. Pomeroy had stated that he would like to see a monthly ceremony of this description. He did not know whether Capt. Pomeroy was in the secret but one of the questions which had arisen lately was how many ships the company could lay down at the same time and the reply of the manager was "ten" (Applause). This

The steam hammer of the Bute Shipbuilding, Engineering and Dry Dock Company. 1884.

SS Collivaud built 1884 by the Bute Shipbuilding Engineering and Dry Dock Company in Clifton Gorge.

would not be far off one a month and he hoped to see the time when that number of ships would be built at the same time (Hear! hear!). There was no reason why Cardiff owners should go to the North for their ships. The steel of which the *Cardiff Castle* and the vessel now on the stocks was built had been manufactured not far from Cardiff and it had been delivered much cheaper in the yard than steel manufactured in the North could be delivered in the Northern yards (Applause). The difference was something like 25/ – per ton and that was an important matter in connection with ship building. He was not going to make a political speech or refer to the many things that had been said lately as to the Union of workmen but he was glad to say that the secretary of the men's Union had placed Cardiff on the same standard as the Tyne and the Clyde and the consequence was that, after a slight difference in regard to matters of detail they had been able at Cardiff to build ships at the same wages as in the North. This was a matter that was now being examined in Cardiff and he was pleased that all differences had been settled in as much as the wages were now exactly the same as on the Tyne and Clyde. Having the steel close at hand and men able and willing to work at the same wages as in the North there was no reason why Cardiff ships should not be built at that port. The Dowlais steel would compare very favourably with — indeed, he would go so far as to say it was far superior to — that used in the North. Coming from the Midlands the other day he was surprised to hear a gentleman state that he could not use the scrap iron of which ships were built in the North for forging purposes on account of the bad quality. The steel from the Dowlais Works was good enough to use for any forging purposes and consequently the ships built at Cardiff were far superior to those built in the North. He thought that in these circumstances the Cardiff ships should obtain a higher class at Lloyds. (Loud Applause).'

Shortly after the ceremony was performed Mr. Farrell received a note from Sir William Thomas Lewis in which he expressed the pleasure it would give him to distribute £10 among the men employed in the yard.

Philip and Martha Morel did not attend the launching but their eldest daughter, Maud, was the Miss Morel of Lavernock who presented the bouquet. The newspaper report omitted to mention that immediately after the launching the vessel collided with the Clarence Road Bridge over the Taff which was under construction at the time.

The *Western Mail* reporter stated that the *Cardiff Castle* was the eighth ship that had been launched from that particular yard on the River Taff.

Despite Captain Pomeroy's optimistic forecast and Thomas Morel's no less optimistic reply, the Bute Shipbuilding, Engineering and Dry Dock Company was unable to place a firm order for steel for their next ship with the Dowlais Iron Co.

'7th December, 1889

To E.P. Martin.

Dear Sir

. . . . re the delay in giving you specifications and I do not propose to delay them indefinitely. In fact if necessary I should at once instruct Mr. Rennie to send up specifications for the building of a duplicate of No. 8. If therefore it is necessary for you to have the specifications please say at once and same will be attended to. We should have the angle irons to go on with so that the platers finishing No. 9 would go on with the new work.

Yours faithfully,
Thos. Morel.'

The Dowlais Iron Co. pressed for the specifications but on 4th February 1890, Morel Brothers were unable to send them up as 'they had been with Lloyds since the beginning of January and Lloyds were under such pressure having changed their rules that they had not, up till then, been able to approve the specification'. In March, the specifications have not been submitted and there was a complication in that Thomas Morel had an interview with Sir William Thomas Lewis over the position of the Bute Shipbuilding Yard. It would seem, although the reasons for this are unclear, that there was a suggestion that Morel Brothers themselves should take over the Bute Shipbuilding Yard. In a letter of 13th March Thomas Morel wrote to E.P. Martin:

> '. . . . it was decided that we should delay taking the Bute Shipbuilding Yard over for the present for reasons which Sir William Thomas Lewis will be able to explain to you when you meet.
>
> This, of course, will necessitate delay in sending you specifications. I quite see that it is not fair to have this order on your Books which you cannot execute at present and should propose dealing with the matter in the same manner as we have dealt with on carriage contracts, i.e. to cancel same.'

In a note in pencil written by a Dowlais Iron Company official are the words: 'Break off further negotiations'.

This they did, notwithstanding that Thomas Morel made very great efforts to ensure that the Dowlais Company did not suffer from the loss of the contract. He acted as a middleman to secure the placement of a near identical order for the steel for a ship for T.R. Oswald & Co. of Milford Haven. Thomas Morel forwarded this order in full detail having obtained acceptance of the price. He wrote:

> 'it is understood that if you do business with this firm for a limited quantity we should make arrangements with the Bank of Gloucester for the payment. We are not ourselves in the least interested and only transmit you this matter as we receive it in view of the postponement of the delivery of our order.'

As not infrequently happens on the breakdown of negotiations the parties started to abuse each other. Thomas Morel went to the Imperial Hotel, Torquay and a letter from E.P. Martin followed him there. Its contents can be guessed from Thomas's replies to the Dowlais Company. In the first:

> 'I must protest against your statement that my offer to cancel has come from the fact that prices of steel have fallen — it's nothing of the sort and I cannot for a single moment admit such a position.'

He then made the statement quoted earlier about pushing forward the development of shipbuilding in Cardiff adding finally:

> 'I have received no encouragement but insults and misrepresentations.'

The second reply followed close on the heels of the first:

Imperial Hotel,
Torquay
20th March, 1890

> Dear Sirs,
>
> I enclose a note from Mr. Oswald of Milford. I am very desirous to make it clear that you have suffered no loss through the cancelment of the contract by my firm and should again point out to you that I am not a merchant wishing to make a profit on a contract, this purchase (sic) has been made to continue ship building at Cardiff which has, I regret to say, now received a death blow.
>
> Yours truly,
> Thomas Morel'

The SS *Mayfield* was launched a month later on 19th April, 1890 at 6.30a.m. The *South Wales Daily News* carried a full account of the launching. The vessel was christened by Maud Morel and her father Philip and Thomas Morel were present at the launch, but neither attended the champagne breakfast afterwards. The owners expressed their satisfaction with the ship, Mr. Woods saying that:

> '. . . though the Mayfield has been a long time building he was very much pleased with her now believing that he had got a perfect ship. He had built on the Clyde and at Stockton and the East Coast but this steamer was second to none that had been turned out at these ports.'

The newspaper report also carried the following comment:

> 'We understand the owners are so well pleased with the build and general workmanship of the steamer that they are prepared to give the Bute Shipbuilding Company an order for a duplicate ship. The only hesitation the Firm has about accepting the order is the uncertainty connected with the workmen. Owing to so much repairing having to be done in Cardiff and the comparatively limited number of platers, riveters, etc. resident in the port, there is a certain difficulty in keeping men in new work, the old being so much more remunerative. Consequently it would hardly be safe for the Company to promise early delivery when they are not in a position to compete with firms who lay themselves out, as in the Tyne, Clyde and other rivers, for shipbuilding only.'

The fact that the Morel family was absent from the champagne breakfast after the launching of the *Mayfield*, although Maud had actually christened the ship, must have reflected the gloom felt by Thomas Morel and expressed in his last letter to the Dowlais Company of the lack of any future for the Bute Shipbuilding Yard. Thomas Morel was not one to let pass an occasion for publicising the services of the companies with which he was identified; but he and his brother were not willing to be present at what might well have been an embarrassing occasion when the emphasis would inevitably be on the launching of the new vessel which they had reason to believe would be the last.

M.J. Daunton marshalls the arguments that have been put forward to explain why Cardiff never became the ship building centre that many had predicted. He lists the short leases granted by the Bute estate, high wages, 'union obstructiveness', lack of capital and of entrepreneurs with a local loyalty, and the absence of supporting works to serve as an industrial base for the industry.[1]

The history of the attempt by the Morels to establish ship building in Cardiff reveals the presence of a number of these factors. There was clearly some difficulty with the lease of the Yard from the Bute estate and there had been problems over wages, which at the launching of the *Cardiff Castle* Thomas Morel suggested had been solved.

The lack of a manufacturing base in and around Cardiff was serious. Although the Company owned the Treherbert Foundry and Engineering Works which could supply some of the castings needed it could not supply the ships' engines; for these the Company had to go to Kemp in Glasgow or to Palmers in Jarrow. Messrs Harland and Wolff in a somewhat similar situation in Belfast, having had to tow ships to the Clyde to be engined, decided in 1880 that their future could not be secured unless they built their own engine works, as they did, to manufacture all the machinery for their vessels. This solution was not adopted in Cardiff.

Thomas Morel had access to capital, as he had indicated to the Dowlais Iron Co. and his identification with Cardiff could not be questioned but he could not persuade that Company to go along with his ideas. He was perhaps over optimistic in his expectation that the Dowlais Company would 'make such a low offer that would enable the Bute Shipbuilding Company to undertake the building of a boat or two', in the expectation that several orders would follow to the ultimate advantage of the Dowlais Iron Co. From Thomas Morel's point of view it was this lack of imagination on the part of the Dowlais Company together with the policy of the Bute estate over leases that dealt shipbuilding at Cardiff its 'death blow'.

There were two additional factors. Firstly, the Morels were engaged in a number of ploys and they must have missed the support of John Angel Gibbs who would have been party to the planning of the Bute Shipbuilding, Engineering and Dry Dock Company but who did not live to see its realization.

Secondly, a major part of their Company's activity was its ship repairing, which Daunton notes as being so much more remunerative than shipbuilding. The Bute Dry Dock off the Roath Basin was one of the graving docks which made Cardiff probably the most important ship repairing centre in the Country. Ships arriving at Cardiff in ballast could conveniently enter dry dock for repairs before obtaining a cargo of coal which would be readily available when repairs were completed. In March 1886, the 'special commissioner' mentioned that the Bute Dry Dock could accommodate four vessels for repairing at any one time and that on the occasion of his visit 'there were two fine steamers being repaired and another was expected that evening', adding 'during twelve months this dock has berthed for repairs over 200 vessels. The dry dock at present employs 500 employees whose wages bill last week was over £550.'

Thomas expected too much of the Dowlais Company. Committed as they were to shipbuilding, the Morels had not sufficient financial resources themselves to undergird it, for example, in the same way that Palmers of Jarrow were able to undergird their business. The methods of payment for ships built by them, as Edward Holden had described, was by giving extended credit to companies that had ordered ships. Morels were not in a position to do this, especially as the 1890s were, generally, years of depression in shipping and the Firm had suffered a crippling loss at this time.

It is not surprising that the Morels, along with other Cardiff firms, developed their ship repairing rather than continued the struggle to make Cardiff a centre for shipbuilding in South Wales with resources grossly inferior to those of the North East.

INFORMATION FROM THE LLOYDS REGISTER OF BRITISH AND FOREIGN SHIPPING WITH REFERENCE TO THE THREE SHIPS BUILT BY THE BUTE SHIPBUILDING, ENGINEERING AND DRY DOCK COMPANY

SS *Collivaud* was launched in March 1886. The first survey was on 10th July 1885 and the last on 21st June 1886. She was built of Landore steel. A flat keel was specified. Thomas Dobson signed as builder on behalf of the Bute Shipbuilding Company. An Inverted Compound Surface Condensing Engine was fitted and both engine and boiler were made by Palmer & Co. at Newcastle in 1886. The donkey boiler was made at Stockton by Henry Porter. The engines were surveyed at Newcastle. She made her maiden voyage to Alexandria. The SS *Collivaud* remained in service until 1958 when she was broken up.

SS *Cardiff Castle* (Rig: Schooner) was launched on 26th October 1889. The first survey was on 8th November 1888 and the last, 13th November 1889. She was built of steel from the Dowlais Iron and Steel Company. A flat keel was specified. Thomas Dobson signed as builder on behalf of the Bute Shipbuilding Company. A Triple Expansion Engine was fitted, made by William Kemp at Glasgow in 1889. The boilers were made by Anderson and Lyall at Glasgow in the same year. The donkey boiler was made at Stockton by Riley Bros. also in the same year. The engines were surveyed at Glasgow. She made her maiden voyage to Brazil. Her name was changed to the SS *Blaenavon* in 1892. She was eventually mined in 1915.

SS Mayfield (Rig: Schooner) was launched on 19th April 1890. The first survey was on 5th April 1889 and the last, 18th July 1890. She was built of steel, Siemens Martin process, from the Dowlais Iron and Steel Company. No specification as to flat keel was included. The depth from upper part of keel to top of main deck beams was 24-ft. She was constructed with a cellular double bottom and one complete set of sails was supplied. In the Lloyds Survey Records at the Greenwich Maritime Museum full specifications and plans of this ship are preserved. Thomas Dobson signed as builder on behalf of the Bute Shipbuilding Company. A Triple Expansion Engine was fitted, made by William Kemp at Glasgow in 1890; the boilers were made by Anderson and Lyall at Glasgow in the same year. The donkey boiler was made by J. Blake in Manchester also in the same year. The engines were surveyed at Glasgow. Under her owners, Frederick Woods of London, she made her maiden voyage to Alexandria. She was sold in 1903 to the Woodfield Steamship Company. In 1909 she was wrecked whilst on a voyage to the River Clyde from Savona in Italy.

CHAPTER SIX

Morel Limited 1888-1903

In 1888, the Morel brothers were living very comfortably; Philip and Martha with their four children: Maud, Philip Edward, William Gibbs and May, at No. 14 Park Place opposite Cathays Park, in the newly fashionable district of Cardiff, served by the fine new shops of Duke Street and St. Mary Street. Thomas and Susanna, after moving into their second house, in Crockherbtown (now Queen Street) had moved in 1880 to The Lindens in Penarth, with their three elder sons, Thomas Edward (Tom), Ralph Elliott, and Edward Clement, (Clem). Their two youngest children were born there; John Gibbs Gordon Evans and Susan Gladys, shortened to 'Glad' because her parents were delighted to have a daughter. Most of the members of the family were to live in Penarth for some part of their lives.

> 'Penarth was a little village in the middle of the last century with a population of under a hundred. Then in 1859 docks (now closed) were built at the mouth of the Ely, to take the pressure off the overcrowded Cardiff Docks. Terraced housing was built immediately behind for the workers. Soon after came the development of the place under the aegis of the Windsor family, the principal landowners, as a select residential suburb of Cardiff and as a genteel seaside resort . . . above the Esplanade are terraced gardens and higher up stand the large and elaborate mansions of the coal-owners and shipping magnates, in wooded grounds. The atmosphere of this part of Penarth remains strongly and evocatively Victorian.'[1]

The Earl of Plymouth took a personal interest in the development of the town which he had intended to be built entirely of stone and was distressed to discover that brick was being used even for some of the houses in Marine Parade.

In their choice of education for their children the Morels naturally turned to Wesleyan schools. Rydal Mount in Colwyn Bay was chosen for Tom and Philip Edward, the two brothers' eldest sons. This school had been founded in 1885 by T.G. Osborn, formerly Headmaster of Kingswood, the school founded by John Wesley, and 'during the last fifteen years of the nineteenth century the school made for itself a name in Methodism such as no private school for boys had ever before achieved — a family spirit, education of the highest possible order and religious culture.' On leaving school, Tom attended University College, Cardiff for a short period and then entered the family firm in which Philip was already working.

Following John Angel Gibbs's death his estate, when his share in Morel and Company was realised, was considerable enough to make possible his widow's removal to Marine Parade, Penarth. Elizabeth was installed by her brothers-in-law at No. 5 Marine Parade, with her six children, the posthumous son being christened Lidgett after the minister with whom John had worked so closely in

Cathays. In this substantial house — Marine Parade was one of the best town addresses in Wales — Elizabeth struggled to bring up her family. William Benjamin Gibbs, her brother-in-law, had arranged the move so that, living as he did in Penarth, he could help in their upbringing. He relinquished this close oversight, however, after 14 years and moved to Weston-super-Mare from whence, because of the fleet of Campbell Paddle Steamers, he was able to remain in contact with his ship-chandling business at Cardiff Docks either by sea across the Bristol Cannel or by rail if the Channel was too rough or the tides inconvenient. The young Gibbs boys and girls were a handful and their father's influence was greatly missed. For the three elder boys, William, John and Reggie, the Wesleyan Collegiate Institution in Taunton, a 'Middle Class Boarding School for children of Wesleyan parents', later Queen's College, provided a good education. There were also plenty of good opportunities for playing games of which all three took advantage and which they were to continue when they left school at 16 and returned to Penarth — to such effect that the youngest of the three, Reggie, was later capped 15 times for Wales, and never found it easy to combine a life in sport with the demands of a business career. Susanna Morel referred to Elizabeth and her children as 'our Number Five Friends'.

The Philip Morels, having moved further up Park Place to No. 40 (now the Catholic Chaplaincy,) were soon to move again — to Lavernock House overlooking Lavernock Bay beyond Penarth. This was but a stepping stone to moving into Penarth itself in 1895 to the large red brick house standing in four acres of ground at the bottom of Marine Parade which Philip built for himself and named with conscious pride: 'Penarth House'. Martha, his wife, was of a somewhat frivolous turn of mind. This was evident even in old age when as an avid bridge player, her opening call was almost invariably 'Try a no trump!' She was mistress of a prestigious house. The reception rooms were magnificent, the drawing-room being furnished in Louis XV style. Although less than 50 yards from the cliff top, the view of the Bristol Channel was obtainable only from the maids' bedrooms on the third floor.

Thomas Morel, not content with his town house, The Lindens, planned and built a large country house for himself at St. Andrews. St. Andrews House, for so it was named, was little further from Cardiff by road than was Penarth and was also served by a railway station at Dinas Powis, some two miles away. The whole family and household moved there each summer from the month of May onwards and returned to Penarth in the autumn.

Here Thomas could farm and the children could ride. It was a move into, but not very far into, the County and it gave the boys a taste of living in the country and introduced them to country pursuits — hunting, point to point racing and shooting, which, apart from the staid eldest son Tom, they were to follow keenly all their lives.

St Andrew's House, St Andrews, Dinas Powis. Built by Thomas Morel in 1892.

Penarth House, Penarth, built by Philip Morel in 1895.

Thomas's relationships with his sons were those of the traditional Victorian father; windows they had broken were mended before he returned from the office so that the damage could be kept from him. Although French was his native tongue, he did not converse with his children in French, with the result that, when Clem went to Rydal School at 18 as a senior pupil, the headmaster noted 'he seemed to know nothing of French at all'. Probably Thomas did not in any case talk much with his children; he had little time left from his business and his public duties for family life.

Susanna was of a more serious frame of mind than her sister Martha. She took an especial interest in the building of the new Wesleyan chapel, Trinity, which was as different from the other Methodist chapels of this period as the Anglican architect could make it, although the Trustees, of whom Thomas was one, would not have considered calling it 'Holy' Trinity. A handsome building with raked floor and seating 600 people without a gallery, it was conceived in the late Gothic style and proclaimed that the Wesleyans were at least of equal status socially and religiously with the members of the Anglican Church.

The Lindens domestic staff was female. Susanna did not aspire to a servants' hall presided over by a butler, but 'outside' there was a coachman and groom and gardeners, who were Thomas's responsibility.

The carriage took Thomas to his office at the Docks, Susanna to the shops in Cardiff, and the whole family to Trinity Church. During the service the coachman and groom would wait outside until worship was over and then take the family home again.

Trinity had a large congregation, many of whom were wealthy and although the Wesleyan ministers stationed there never stayed, as was the pattern, for more than three years, they lived comfortably on a Wesleyan minister's stipend with one or two servants — in typical middle-class style. The most prominent of them was the Rev. Robert Bond, later to become Secretary of the Wesleyan Conference and a frequent visitor to The Lindens where he would play billiards with the young members of the family.

On 26th March, 1888 the *Western Mail* carried the announcement that:

> 'Messrs. Morel Bros. and Co., Cardiff, steamship owners and managers and ship and insurance brokers, Cardiff has just been converted into a limited liability company with a capital of £500,000 in £100 shares. According to the terms of registration the purchase consideration was £499,400 in fully paid shares and the subscribers were: Philip Morel, 2497 shares, Thomas Morel 2497 shares and Martha Angel Morel, Maud Alys Morel, Philip Edward Morel, Susanna Elliot Angel Morel, Thomas Edward Morel and Thomas Morel, 1 share each. The vendors were appointed directors and managers.'

The holdings of the two Morel families were exactly equal, Thomas Morel's extra share balancing that of his niece, Maud. Philip and Thomas, the vendors, became joint Directors and Managers. At the first meeting of the Directors on

12th May at their registered office, 2 Stuart Street, a call for the full amount of the shares was made and share certificates were issued for the fully paid shares.

The move into a limited liability status was in line with the growing resources of the Firm and to counter the possible threat which the unlimited liability of their former partnership had posed. Previously each partner was fully responsible in law for the financial activities of the others and the liability, if anything went seriously wrong in the business, was total. By becoming a Limited Company they were moving into line with other comparable commercial undertakings. It brought no particular tax advantages, but removed the threat that the failure or unwise action of one partner might have disastrous consequences for all the members of the partnership.

During this time, the two commodities with which Morels were concerned almost exclusively continued to be coal and ore. Some ten letters in the Dowlais Iron Company collection of this period are concerned with developments in the importing of iron ore. In 1889, Thomas Morel offered Rubio ore from Bilbao at 12/6 a ton making a special price 'because we have the direction of the steamers in hand'. In the same year another steel producing firm, the Forest Company, was 'choked with ore and delaying our ship' and Thomas Morel asked Dowlais 'to take 1000 tons and repay them later from one of your ships'. There was criticism of delay at the Dowlais Orcorera wharf in Bilbao. The Morel ship arrived there on the 22nd of April and did not get away until 1st May. Thomas Morel wrote: 'This delay is ruinous'.

Almost casually, a memorandum dated 10th October, 1889 noted that 'we have received a message from our Mr. T. Morel from Birmingham confirming the carriage of 175,000 tons of ore from Bilbao to Cardiff over 1890, we shall no doubt have particulars from him tomorrow and will write you further'.

It was, however, not only with Dowlais and the other South Wales companies that the Morels were trading. Freights were fixed with Dunlop and Co., Clyde Ironworks, Glasgow, Walkers of Tyne and the Steel Company of Scotland at figures that differed considerably. Frequently, the Morels showed their wish to be identified with South Wales. In 1894 Thomas Morel wrote of the ore which he was importing from Almeria in Southern Spain; 'Middlesborough will take all they can get of it at 12/6 a ton', however, 'I am anxious that the ore should come to this neighbourhood' and he made an offer of 10/9 to Dowlais. The manager in the Dowlais works office pencilled a note, 'accept one cargo', which seems a somewhat grudging response.

In June 1890, Morels wrote to Dowlais about ore from Greece:

> 'We are offered the output of the Iron Ore mine at Seriphos — the ore as you are aware has given universal satisfaction. We feel inclined to place some special ships suitable for this trade to import the ore into the United Kingdom. We have gone carefully into figures and although the freight is low before the new crop of grain is harvested it is quite impossible to import the ore under 14/ – , free on board, at

> Cardiff. I enclose telegram from our London House offering us 7/9 Seriphos to Tyne; for your guidance we have placed the freight at 6/9 for Cardiff. This is a very low freight indeed from a Greek port.'

The lower freight quoted above for Cardiff compared with Tyne would be possible because of the shorter distance from Seriphos and the ease of getting a freight 'out' without the need for a voyage from Newcastle to Cardiff in ballast.

The Firm was expert at deciding the price at which the ore was to be offered at a United Kingdom port. This depended on the cost of the ore in its country of origin, the efficiency and characteristics of the ports involved, the distance, if any that the ships would need to sail in ballast, and the freight which they could obtain or for which they needed to allow when using their own ships.

The carrying of ore continued to be the major importing activity of the Morels during this period and with such contracts as that for 175,000 tons with Dowlais in 1890 they had no need to diversify. Bringing ore into Cardiff and carrying coal out was the lucrative routine for the Firm.

The Firm was ever anxious, even to the extent of going to law, to avoid unnecessary expenditure — especially in paying demurrage for any delays in the discharging of the ships.

Before the Court of Appeal in July 1891 Morel Brothers sought to establish that a company who had chartered one of their vessels was responsible for the costs resulting from delay before the vessel could be berthed, due to the crowded state of the Garston docks high up the Mersey.

The matter turned on the interpretation of when the voyage had been completed. The Morels maintained that their responsibility ceased when the berth was ordered by the harbour master, although it was not immediately available. The charterers did not accept responsibility until the ship was able to be discharged.

The Court ruled that it was the shipowners who had to take responsibility for any delay that occurred before the ship could be berthed and discharging begin. The Morels' claim was thus not sustained and a judgment given which, if profit margins had been tight, could have had serious repercussions both for them and for other shipowners.

In October 1892, Morel Brothers protested to the Cardiff Town Council, although the matter did not become a legal issue, about the delay occasioned by their S.S. *Merthyr* being unable to reach a coal tip at the dockside as the *Champion*, which had been hired in connection with the prevention of cholera, was alongside in their berth at the time. The Medical Officer maintained that the *Merthyr* could not, in fact, have entered the docks as the gates were then closed.

The matter was not pressed further. However, it illustrates how the Firm did not suffer delays gladly even at their home port and in a cause so identified with the health of the whole community as the prevention of cholera.

With a new company structure it might have been expected that Morel Limited, when the second rapid growth in shipping in Cardiff occurred between 1897 and 1919, would maintain their leading position in the Docks that they had held as Morel Brothers in the period up to 1884. This was not to be and the reasons lay paradoxically partly in the size of the fleet with which they entered into the 1890s, and partly with personal factors within the Firm itself.

To the boom conditions of 1897, '. . . existing Companies were able to adapt, but the development, first of steamships generally and then of specialized vessels for the coal trade did give newcomers a chance to exploit the development without having to write off old capital . . . and the relative ease of raising capital permitted a second generation of shipowners to emerge to dominance. While the first generation of leaders did not decline absolutely, it did relatively and in the second phase of growth was surpassed by newcomers such as W.J. Tatem, Edward Nicholl, William Reardon Smith and Evan Thomas, Radcliffe. These firms experienced quite remarkable growth in the late 1890s.' [2]

The personal factors are complex; whilst at the beginning of this period of growth both Philip and Thomas Morel were in their prime and well versed in shipping practice and their two elder sons were coming into the management of the Company, they already were very wealthy men with a large house and farm apiece. Failure, if there were to be failure, would be spectacular — and the way down would be a long fall.

The new men who were to take over leadership in the early 1900s had everything to gain and little, if anything, to lose if their shipping enterprises came to naught.

Another factor lay in the contrasting nature of the two brothers. As was appropriate for the elder brother, Philip chaired both Morel Limited and the Bute Docks Shipbuilding, Engineering and Dry Dock Company, but he did not have his brother's drive in public and political matters. He was a Liberal in politics, which was to be expected of a Wesleyan of his day, and served on the Cardiff Town Council, but only for three years. An article in *Men of the Period* lists his commercial commitments; 'a member of the Chamber of Shipping, Chamber of Commerce and the Cardiff Exchange, the Baltic Committee and Lloyds Committee and Director of the Cardiff Paper Mill Company. He was a member of the Cardiff Naturalists Society and took an active interest in the Volunteer movement. His listed hobby is the study of architecture.' By no means an introvert, he was considerably less outgoing than his younger brother.

The brothers' temperaments influenced their activities with the Firm; Philip remained for the most part in Cardiff whilst Thomas visited Spain frequently to develop the mining interest there.

For Thomas, it almost seemed that shipping ceased to be his main interest — certainly, he had surplus energy for other activities. He entered politics. He had been for a long period Chairman of the Cardiff Pilotage Board as well as serving his term as President of the Cardiff Shipowners Association and of the Cardiff Chamber of Commerce. His sympathies were wide enough to include being President for a number of years of the Cardiff Cymmrodorion Society.

Attracted by the possibility of getting to Cardiff Docks from Penarth by water, he founded a ferry service from Penarth for this purpose. The three ferry boats: *Iona, Kate*, and *Belle Marie* sailed direct from Penarth slipway to the pierhead in Cardiff. He actually owned the *Iona*.

For Philip, the achievements of Morel Limited were enough; for Thomas, they might have been but the lower rungs of a ladder.

The Minute Book of Morel Ltd. is preserved, but it is tantalisingly lacking in details of the day to day life of the Company. At the early Annual General Meetings from 1889 to 1903 dividends were declared of between 1¼% to 7½% with amounts carried forward of between £1,159 and £9,619.

In 1892 and 1893, the loss of £9,000 on the sale of the SS *Ninian Stuart* was written off and in 1893, £865 on the sale of the SS *Cardiff*. In 1894, first debenture bonds of £50,000 were handed to Philip and Thomas Morel in part payment of amounts due to them for dividends.

There is an indication here of what was to become a permanent feature of Morel Ltd; more money in the Firm than the amounts the directors wished to disburse by way of dividends.

In 1896, at an Extraordinary Meeting of Morel Ltd., the Articles of Association were altered, Philip and Thomas Morel 'having made arrangement with their eldest sons', so that both Philip E. and Tom were formally appointed Directors and Managers of the Management Company.

In 1896 the Annual General Meeting passed the following resolution: 'That as it is imperative for the efficient working of the freights, insurance and other matters connected with the steamers managed by the Company that one director should reside in London by turn of not less than three years duration and as the expense of residence in London is considerably in excess of Cardiff the annual sum of £100 shall be paid to said resident in London'.

None of the four directors, however, did move to London and the Firm had to be content with the opening of a London office in Leadenhall Buildings, E.C. of which C.J. Hill was the first Manager.

From 1897 onwards the Firm's writing paper in addition to the 2 Stuart Street Cardiff address carried: 'and at Leadenhall Buildings, London E.C. and 123 Docks Street, Newport, Mon.'

Thomas Morel engaged in ventures outside the owning, managing and chartering of ships, entering as we have noted into local undertakings on a considerable scale. Philip agreed that Morel Limited should accept responsibility for his brother's part in some of these ventures, in which it seemed that Thomas had overreached himself. This brotherly action was appreciated by Thomas's sons, aware of their father's propensity to take risks. Large sums were guaranteed in 1900 to Lloyds Bank for Thomas Morel's part in the Prince of Wales Dry Dock at Swansea, and the Firm assumed responsibility for his commitment in the New Cardiff Milling Company, and for the promotion of the New Graving Dock in the New Cardiff Docks, then being built.

Whilst the relationships between the Morels seem to have been good, the relationship between the Morels and the Gibbs, however, remained strained. Evidence of this exists in a letter from Susanna Gibbs to her son-in-law Thomas Morel. She had asked for a contribution to the Methodist cause in Portland and he must have replied enclosing £50, but writing in derogatory terms of her sons' business dealings with him. She answered:

> 'Dear Sir,'
>
> I am obliged on behalf of the cause in Portland for the cheque for £50 you have sent me and I will send it on. I am sorry you should think as you do in reference to my sons and I feel sure you have made a mistake. If they had treated you unkindly I should not have approved of it and I never heard anyone else charge them with unkindness. As to your paying them a large sum of money, I suppose if you had not dealt with them you would have paid it to someone else and they must have been of some assistance to you when you were getting up business in your Dry Dock. As to your later treatment of them I have never before heard of Dry Docks coming between relatives. What a pity you have let all these years pass with such feelings on your mind that could have been cleared up in a moment.
>
> Yours sincerely,
> Susanna Gibbs'

It would seem that Thomas had referred in his letter to the fact that the halting progress of the Bute Shipbuilding, Engineering and Dry Dock Company was due in his mind to its being starved of capital, and that the need to find money from within Morel Brothers and Company for the John Angel Gibbs Estate was a factor in the failure of the shipbuilding enterprise: he must have accused the Gibbs family of, at least, 'unkindness'.

Susanna was understandably unable to comprehend the full significance of the effect of her son John Angel's early death on the relationships within the Firm.

The tension further showed itself in a letter written by Thomas to his wife, Susanna, undated, but probably around 1889 when he was on what seems a holiday trip in Mid Wales:

> 'My dear wife,
>
> I have your letter — I am sorry I have caused you pain and I had a thought to tear up my last letter instead of sending it — but after all it is better to speak

plain. I note what you say about your people not speaking ill of me; it's just what I complain of, if they had done that I could have answered but they act behind our back still professing to be friendly.

Mr. Cory told me matters which I would never have thought of — what I complain of most is that you do not seem to desire so much of my company but are perfectly satisfied to be with those who have insulted and injured your husband — be sure this is wrong and you reap the fruits by being unhappy. We did not write yesterday, we went for a drive and it was too late when we came to the hotel.

We shall start again for Aberystwyth. Write us there, care of the Lion Hotel. If it was wet I should return from there by train as you seem to be comfortable. I think it would be as well to cut my trip shorter and have some time with you. The boys are enjoying themselves well. Ralph seems much better, of course it's a great treat for him.

Your affection husband,
Thomas Morel

Kiss Clem, Gladys and John.'

Strong feelings there were, but also strong contacts as well. Ralph went in 1892, not long after this letter was written, to school at Queen's College, Taunton, where his cousins William and John Angel Gibbs already were pupils, and the youngest Morel son, John, went to Rydal College with Lidgett, the youngest of the Gibbs boys. However, when William and John Angel Gibbs junior entered commerce on leaving school, neither of them went into their late father's firm to work with their Morel cousins, as did John Morel, son of Jean. This was the more noticeable as the Firm numbered on its staff two young Portlanders, Richard Hinde and Clem Scriven, who would have owed their position to Martha or Susanna speaking for them.

Despite this, there was plenty of coming and going between the younger generation of Morels and Gibbs, both at home and away from home, even if the senior members still nursed their grievances.

CHAPTER SEVEN

Thomas Morel

Thomas Morel was more than one of the founding partners of Morel Limited. In contrast to all the other docksmen of his period, he identified himself with the civic life of Cardiff from the time he was first elected as councillor for the South Ward in 1885. He continued to serve on the town council, becoming an alderman in 1898 and mayor in 1899. He stood as a Conservative, unusual for a Wesleyan of his day, although at that time the local policies of that party were never easily distinguishable from those of the Liberals. The Conservatives might favour economy rather than expenditure, but they were the Party pressing for 'new docks' rather than the Liberal, 'no more docks', and they accepted, with the Liberals, that the provision of services was a proper municipal function — if such were economically and effectively run.

At the opening of the Splott Bridge in 1899, Thomas expressed his view of municipal government and how it should be related to the Imperial Parliament:

> 'The force and foresight of the elected representatives had given Cardiff pure water and plenty of it, wide streets, plenty of lung spaces second to none in the United Kingdom, splendid free libraries, sanitoria and other conveniences, while electric trams and other good things were to come. In short, "municipalism" had given Cardiff the prime necessities of life . . . The Imperial Parliament had now more than it could do. It often bothered itself with things that might very well be left to them at Cardiff. Why should they have to incur the cost and delay of going to Westminster to purchase tram lines and carry out other matters? This sort of thing was an anachronism of the nineteenth century at which future generations would smile. He would welcome in the future a wider field of local self-government. This would leave municipalities absolutely free to work out their own social salvation in every respect.'

In 1899 Thomas Morel, as Mayor of Cardiff, signed the agreement with the Bute Estate to purchase Cathays Park for £158,000, to serve as the site for the new Town Hall and other public buildings. There followed a programme of major civic expenditure which included extension to the tramways, the construction of a new sewer and the building of the new asylum at Whitchurch. On 20th March, 1899 Thomas Morel opened Cathays Park to the public.

His property interests in Cardiff were small; his ownership of No. 2 Stuart Street gave him a property qualification and he was a dry dock proprietor, but alone amongst the elite of coal owners and ship owners — and with as heavy commercial responsibilities as any — he was prepared to spend a considerable time on the meetings of the Council, and on the five sub committees on which he served, being Chairman of the Finance Committee for a period.

As a spokesman for the town his words carried weight. In 1898 he was called to give evidence to the Inspector, Major General Philip Carey, at the Local Government Board Enquiry into the proposed extension of the boundary of the Borough of Cardiff to include the whole of Penarth and the districts of the north and west of Cardiff. Thomas Morel was in favour of Cardiff taking in Penarth.

His status as a witness was established by Francis Williams appearing on behalf of Cardiff; 'a magistrate, a shipowner', 'his Firm; the largest shipowners in Cardiff', 'carrying on his business in Cardiff whilst living in Penarth and having another residence at Dinas Powis', 'well acquainted with the district having lived in it since 1866'.

His Cardiff interests were also established; 'a member of the Cardiff Town Council since 1885 and a large ratepayer in the Borough'.

Thomas Morel's case for the incorporation of Penarth into Cardiff rested on two premises; firstly, 'that the people who resided in Penarth were mainly Cardiff people' and, secondly, 'that the coal exported from Penarth Docks was Cardiff coal'.

He evidenced the first point by indicating that 'most of the people who lived in Penarth worked, shopped and came for their amusements in Cardiff.'

The second point he established was that 'if coal was sold as Penarth Coal rather than Cardiff Coal it would depreciate it 6d. to 1/ – a ton. If a shipowner were offered Penarth Coal he would say "We don't want Penarth Coal we want Cardiff Coal" '. He had to admit, however, that, in fact, it came from the Rhondda Valley and also that the coal that passed through the port of Barry was also called Cardiff Coal. There was no move to incorporate Barry into Cardiff. This illustrated the weakness of his argument from the actual name of the coal which had, in fact, become a brand name from whatever port it was exported.

Although Thomas continued to maintain that Cardiff and Penarth were one for business purposes and should be one for municipal purposes, the Inspector ruled otherwise. The two areas continued to be separately administered and Cardiff was unable to appropriate the rateable value of Penarth to itself.

Probably no one could have won this particular battle. The great majority of Penarth residents had no wish to be swamped by Cardiff and they have successfully resisted being incorporated into Cardiff at all subsequent enquiries.

Thomas Morel was very much a public figure in Cardiff, both at the docks and in the Council Chamber and his commitment to the town, not of his birth but of his adoption, was recognized nationally in 1899. Queen Victoria conferred on him a Knighthood on 30th June at Windsor Castle. The Prime Minister, Lord Salisbury, had written by hand on Foreign Office paper: 'The Queen has been graciously pleased to approve of a submission that I have made to Her Majesty that you should receive the Honour of a Knighthood on the occasion of Her Majesty's Birthday. I feel sure that this announcement will be

Morel Limited offices. No 2 Stuart Street, Cardiff Docks taken in 1972, shortly before demolition.

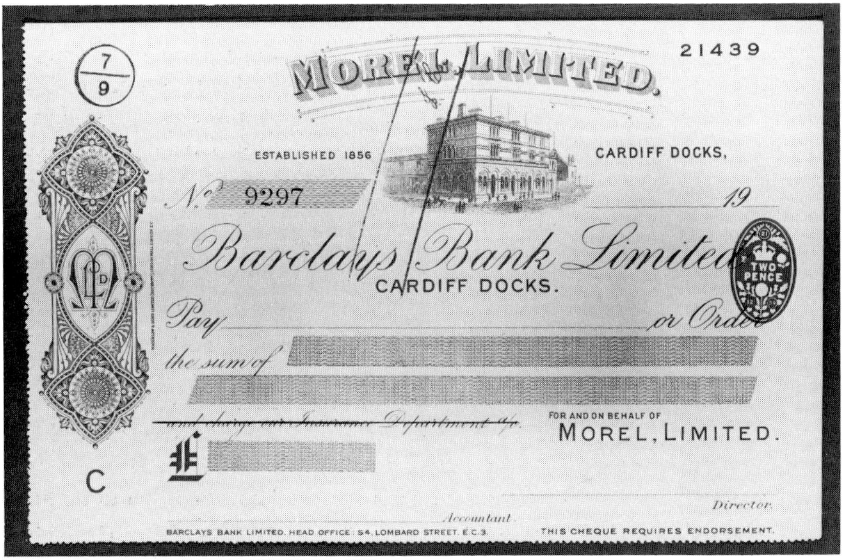

7/9

21439

MOREL, LIMITED.

ESTABLISHED 1856

CARDIFF DOCKS,

No 9297

19

Barclays Bank Limited

CARDIFF DOCKS.

TWO PENCE

Pay or Order

the sum of

~~and charge our Insurance Department a/c~~

FOR AND ON BEHALF OF

MOREL, LIMITED.

£

C

Accountant.

Director.

BARCLAYS BANK LIMITED. HEAD OFFICE: 54, LOMBARD STREET. E.C.3.

THIS CHEQUE REQUIRES ENDORSEMENT.

Facsimile of cheque used by Morel Limited at the beginning of the century.

extremely welcome to all classes of the great community of which you are the head.' The Home Office supplied details of dress — 'ordinary morning dress (frock coat)' and indicated that Thomas Morel should travel to Windsor by train 'leaving Paddington at 1.10p.m. Luncheon will be provided at the Castle'.

Thomas Morel made the journey to Windsor and returned to Cardiff as Sir Thomas. It was customary, but by no means obligatory, for a newly created Knight to petition the College of Heralds for a Grant of Arms. Sir Thomas chose rather to devise his own Coat of Arms with some anonymous assistance. The result was infelicitous. The fact that he was a shipowner was symbolised acceptably enough by the ship carried on the shield, the three supporting Tudor Roses were conventional run-of-the-mill heraldic symbols but the motto: 'Pugna Pro Patria', was quite inappropriate for a man of peace who had largely cut himself off from his own birthplace. At about the same time his brother, Philip, also had a coat of arms devised, without the help of the College. The shield, blazoned with three quatrefoils, the crest, a dexter arm in armour, embowed, the hand holding a rose, slipped. He chose as his motto 'Semper fidelis'.

A Complimentary Banquet was held on Thursday, 6th July, 1899 at the Town Hall in Cardiff to recognize Sir Thomas's honour. Tickets were 12/6. There were speeches and a musical programme at which the accompanist was Madame Clara Novello Davies, a prominent figure in Welsh musical circles at this period.

During the proposing of Sir Thomas's health, the chairman, the Member of Parliament for Cardiff, could not resist making a political speech, referring 'at some length to the Transvaal question' as the *Western Mail* report had it. In his speech Thomas Morel set down his political aims; 'To promote the welfare of the town and port. Let the wealth and power of the Docks associate and become identified with the public life of the town; the docksmen taking the full share of responsibility in municipal work and enterprises, thus fulfilling their duties as citizens and ensuring the future prosperity and progress of the town. There is an immediate, bright and glorious future for the town'.

The chairman noted that Cardiff was the only town that had been selected for the honour of having its Mayor chosen to be appointed to the dignity of knighthood, and it may well be that the honour was political in that the Conservative Party on the Council was pressing the popular cause that the town should become a city with the status that this implied. The Knighthood recognized the growing importance of Cardiff and anticipated its actually becoming a city early in the twentieth century. Sir Thomas Morel underlined this point: 'He felt a certain amount of pride that Cardiff, not himself, had been so graciously recognized'. He made a stirring call for unity; 'As a

View from Morel Limited offices of the entrance to Cardiff Docks, taken in 1972.

commercial man I strongly exhort the whole of the forces in Cardiff to closely unite'.

This hope for a glorious future would not have been realized if Cardiff had continued to rely for its prosperity almost solely on the export of coal, with which many were contented in 1900. He could not have foreseen that, in the main, shunning diversification, Cardiff would survive only because her claim to be the capital of Wales was accepted, howbeit grudgingly in some quarters. As administration has largely taken over from commerce, so the centre of activity has moved from the Docks towards Cathays Park. The Coal and Shipping Exchange has long since closed, and in the first week of January, 1980, there was only one ship in the whole complex of Cardiff Docks and she was of Far Eastern registration. However, specialized berths for cargoes such as packaged timber, fruit and refined petroleum are now available, and two-storied houses, with modern amenities, are being built again on the cleared areas of Butetown.

In spite of the antagonistic tone of the 'inspired' article in the Liberal paper on the Bute Shipbuilding Engineering and Dry Docks Company which criticised the abnormally short leases granted by the Bute Estate Office, Sir Thomas was not on unfriendly terms with Lord Bute, different as were their backgrounds. Lord Bute regretted that he was unable to be present at the dinner: '. . . along with your other friends', and later he was represented at Sir

Thomas's funeral by Sir William Thomas Lewis.

Thomas Morel's involvement with Cardiff Docks did not prevent him from being also one of the prime movers in developing the Docks at Barry which inevitably challenged the near monopoloy that the Butes had sought to establish in Cardiff. He was very much a South Wales man, totally committed to Cardiff and Glamorgan as an investment area. He eschewed investments in other parts of the United Kingdom and concentrated on those nearer home — which he could keep under review.

He served on the board of directors of a number of these; the Barry Dry Dock and Engineering Company, The Cardiff Railway Company, The Cardiff Paper Mills Company, The Cardiff Grain Company, the *Western Mail* and the Albany, Locketts and Universal Colliery Companies.

The high point of Sir Thomas's mayoral year was the visit of Lord Kitchener to Cardiff to be admitted an Honorary Freeman of the ancient and loyal Borough. The Sirdar of the Egyptian Army, as he was officially known, visited Cardiff on 22nd December, 1899. Out of the £1,000 allowed him by the Council for his year of office, the Mayor provided and was thanked for 'the magnificent hospitality with which he entertained the large number of representatives from all parts of the Principality and for making the gathering one of a Welsh National character'.

Extant is a small shield commemorating this event with miniatures of Lord Kitchener, Sir Thomas and General Gordon, whose death at the hands of the Mahdi in 1885 Lord Kitchener had 'avenged' in the year previous to his visit.

Thomas Morel, as a man, does not emerge in any clarity from the sparse records of his public life. That he was prepared to go further than his statutory obligations required in relieving distress is evidenced by the fact that, in 1898, during the shipping strike of that year when there was considerable withdrawal of tonnage from the port of Cardiff and consequent hardship to the pilots and their families, he took the lead, with Edmund Handcock and other members of the Cardiff Pilotage Board, in advancing money personally to the pilots. The Pilotage Board itself would not, or could not, support them financially. The pilots were able gradually to repay their indebtedness. It was natural that his social concern should be for the welfare of seafarers. He initiated the movement for the erection of a permanent seamen's hospital at the Docks in place of the old hulk, the H.M.S. *Hamadryad*, which did duty for so many years, and he raised a considerable amount of the money for it. He also pressed for the establishment of a school of cookery for ships cooks, which was set up later at Cardiff Docks.

His allegiance to Methodism remained throughout his life. When he attended Loudoun Square Chapel he was Sunday School Superintendent and when he moved to Penarth he was Society Steward at Arcot Street Chapel. Later, with his very considerable public and business duties, it took the form more of trusteeship and of presiding at religious meetings and meetings of social concern. Nevertheless he was a representative to one of the Wesleyan Conferences and a member of the minister's class at Trinity.

His relationships with his brothers were not warm. The rift with Jean was never healed, and with his partner and elder brother, Philip, he was never close except in business dealings in which oftentimes he would take the lead. In the course of the Vero Affair, Thomas wrote to Philip in London on 8th May, 1884:

> . . . I note Vero will be with you tomorrow, no doubt he will be the hardest nut to crack — if he dont accept use all means in your power to give him trouble. . . . Nothing fresh here, matters are taking their usual course. You can therefore use all your thought to this most important question. I hear Dowlais have chartered over next year at 5/ – . I have fixed at 6/1½ for Glasgow. 4/9 less 2% for Newcastle. It will be therefore a great loss for us to take up those shares. Yours truly, Thomas Morel.

Philip did not attend his brother's dinner on 6th July, 1899 possibly because it was largely a Conservative affair. Clem Scriven, a nephew of Elizabeth Gibbs, reported that on Sunday he used to go to No. 5 Marine Parade, Penarth for Sunday dinner which would often be attended by Philip and Martha Morel — never by Thomas and Susanna. Thomas seemed to distance himself from his relatives. His daughters-in-law stood in awe of him. Amy Morel, Ralph's wife, told her daughter how frightened she had been by his steely blue eyes. Christine Nance, daughter of W. Edwin Nance, a Cardiff docksman, and a girlhood friend of Gladys Morel, described him as 'rather on the small size, bright blue eyes, pleasant looks, very charming manner with the ladies; my aunt who was very critical of such things, thought he was charming'. This charm of manner is brought out in an article written, in 1898, in the *Shipping World*: 'Mr. Alderman Morel seems to say nothing without a smile . . . always his face expresses a very sincere amiability as of one who has found life pleasant and wishes to make it pleasant to others'.

Thomas Morel made frequent trips abroad, some on business, some for his health, and he was never accompanied on these by his wife. This was not uncommon for business men at this period. However, he wrote to Susanna frequently and she kept many of these letters. It is from these that a more human picture of Thomas Morel emerges.

The two letters written from St. Mary's in Jersey in 1878 suggest that he was somewhat of a hypochondriac, but he did suffer from poor health and his constant worrying about it may, in itself, have been a factor contributing to his comparatively early death.

St. Mary,
Jersey.

My Dear Wife,

I duly rec'd your second letter and glad to see you are well also our dear boys. My letters will have told you what I do day by day. Yesterday I passed at home and at my sisters. I have hardly been out; town is too far. The weather is so hot that I perspire so freely I fear it is making me very weak. I took medicine for two days which I fear made me very seedy. No post here today. I hope dear Susie to have a letter from you today, we have only delivery three times a week. I don't think I will stay long here, you may expect me at end of next week. I think it is quite necessary to take one flannel shirt off Tom. [ed: his son] This is the cause, I believe, which has made me so delicate. This continuous perspiring must hurt both of us. Sufficient light clothing is what is necessary, do not therefore fail to do what I say; I am certain that it's a mistake to put so much clothes on him. All cases of fatal colds have been caught after being too hot. Kiss the boys for me also kisses for your dear self.

Your affectionate husband,
Thomas Morel.

P.S. Write to me next week, general post office, St. Heliers, Jersey. I shall pass two or three days in town.

St. Mary,
Jersey.

Dear Wife,

I am today in the country the whole day trying to finish my matters and shift in town for a couple of days previous to my starting back.

I am still unwell, but not worse. I am taking quinine to pull up my strength. Have no letters of yours to reply to. Hope you and the boys continue well, kiss them for me. I have a letter from Philip which says that Lizzie is achouched of a girl, all doing well. I had no idea it would be so soon. [ed: Lizzie was Elizabeth Gibbs, wife of John Angel Gibbs. Susan Gibbs was born in 1878.] They are very busy and have passed a contract for building another boat of 1,600 to 1,700 tons burden; this will put our hands very full for several years to come.

It is blowing here rather hard from the S.W. The weather here is much hotter than in England, even the wind is not cold. They say that it is very relaxing.

Your affectionate husband,
Thomas Morel.

Thomas Morel enjoyed going abroad, but homesickness descended on him and usually, if at all possible, he cut short his visits. In Switzerland he stayed at Zermatt in July 1891: 'I had for part of the morning a grand sight, snow hills or mountains on every side with the glaciers down below. I cannot describe the huge waterfalls I have seen . . . I have some goods news to tell you — in fact it is the greatest pleasure I have had for some days and that is that I gave up Chamonix and intend coming right home. I will by this means be back home next week — I am sick and tired of this shifting about. I have my tickets for this Chamonix trip but I shall sacrifice them'.

In February 1892, Thomas Morel went for a holiday to Tenerife and he went on his own. He sailed for Porto Cruz and encounted bad weather on the way which he enjoyed: 'I now don't feel the weather or tossing about one bit. You will notice I claim to be an old salt quite accustomed to the sea.' He travelled on a ship which was going to New Zealand via the Cape of Good Hope and

Sir Thomas Morel in 1899, during his year of office as Mayor of Cardiff.

returning via Cape Horn, 'a very fine ship. I have a large cabin which I share with a Mr. Glode, a retired officer of the Army from Devon, a very nice fellow'. On landing he crossed the Island to Santa Cruz where he stayed at Camarcho's English Hotel. He planned to stay there 10 to 12 days. 'This is not a fast place, no gambling like the Riviera and is therefore more preferable'. By the 5th March he is thinking a lot about home. 'I am now getting homesick again'. About the building of St. Andrews House he wrote: 'Have you driven over to see the house since I left?'. News reaches him of the loss of the Morel ship SS *Blaenavon*, and he wrote on the 6th 'I am trusting to hear that some of the crew have been saved, I cannot make out the cause of her loss, this is quite a mystery'. He contemplated taking a trip to Las Palmas some 35 miles away. 'It is so far to come that I feel it absurd to hurry back.' He continued to think about business and instructed his son, Tom, to send details of the registration of a new ship to the financial editor of the *Western Mail*.

By 10th March, he was really very lonely. 'The worst of this place is that you are completely shut out from your friends.' He described his day:

> 'I go out riding at 7.00 a.m. in the morning and at 4.30 p.m. and sit about during the day when it is too hot to do anything else. We have plenty of music. I read all the time and take life as you see very quietly . . . I hope, dear wife, you are not too lonely, you have the children with you and your friends. Kiss the children for me . . . I want very badly to come home. I am homesick.'

On 11th March he abandoned his plan to go to Las Palmas and sailed for home on the SS *Roma* belonging to the Bristol and African Steam Navigation Company. When he was at sea thirty miles from Madeira he wrote to his son, John:

> 'I am glad to see you are improving in your writing . . . I know you would like to be on board this ship. There are a lot of monkeys — a lot of such queer birds of all kinds coming from the Gold Coast of Africa, also Canary birds from the Canary Islands. When our ships will be sent to these Islands I will instruct the captain to bring you a few. They are very fine indeed and you and Gladys will be all set up with pets — kiss Gladys and Clem for me — from your loving father.'

In August and September of 1901 Thomas took his daughter Gladys, then aged 21, and his youngest son John, aged 18, on a cruise to the Baltic on the steam yacht, the *Argonaut*. At first, Thomas enjoyed the cruise; 'There is plenty of change and plenty to see and what is more valuable plenty of good sea air.' He wrote of his fellow passengers. 'I don't see we have any reason to complain; a lot of clergy and doctors, usual number of widows on the look out for new husbands and the usual number of young girls and young men flirting about the decks.'

The ship stopped at Copenhagen and then sailed on to Kronstadt for St. Petersberg. Thomas decided to make the journey to Moscow. 'It would be a great miss for John and Glad and I must try and bear the journey of 13 hours by train.' He was not well; 'I have been rather worse than when I left, this continual pain after meals — although I am most careful. I dread the Moscow trip.' Moscow, where they stayed at the Hotel Berlin, he found 'a wonderful city, but outside the churches not worth a visit. We have seen sufficient churches and church jewels to last us a lifetime.' After returning to St. Petersberg they sailed for Stockholm. His letters were filled with the desire to get home again and with complaints that he was not receiving letters. 'I have not had a single line from the boys, even from Tom', although he ignored the fact that he did receive letters from his wife at every port. He slept better on board ship than on land but 'the hurry and bustle does not suit me, the anxiety of the children is also too much and the noise and the rattle together with the fatigue has made me ill from my old complaint. . . . It was quite a mistake to undertake the Moscow trip.' Thomas was relieved when the ship took a short cut home through the Baltic Canal, and docked at Tilbury. They caught a train to Dinas Powis and so reached home after a cruise of about three weeks which had been a memorable experience for Gladys and John but far too much for their father, especially the Moscow trip.

A letter survives from a visit Thomas Morel paid to Paris in April 1902. He wrote to Susanna on Sunday after worshipping at the Methodist Chapel in the Rue Roquepine. This Church was a centre for Methodists working in Paris, business men, governesses and nursemaids and its membership included British, Channel Islanders and Americans.

'Grand Hotel Paris
le 19 April, 1902

My dear wife,

I arrived here last night — very tired — glad to have a day of rest. I went to the Rue Roquepine Chapel this morning. Very poor congregation. Paris as usual does not seem to change. The Spring is here and more advanced than with us. I shall, I hope hear from you tomorrow. I shall have three days very hard work and leave on Thursday morning.

I trust you have seen to Collings completing their work.

Your affectionate husband
Thomas Morel'

Thomas Morel went to Almeria in Southern Spain on at least three occasions. These were business trips made in connection with the Gergal Railway and Mines Company which the Morels owned. As the ore mines of the Bilbao region began to be worked out, Thomas Morel explored other sources of usuable ore in the Gergal mountains of Southern Spain.

In March 1898, on the first trip, he sailed on the P & O Ship, the SS *Rome*, and before she left British waters he wrote to his wife. The letter was posted at Ryde.

'My dear Wife,

We are fairly off — clear of the Thames. I am thankful to say clear of fogs — it's very, very cold — but no doubt I will be warmer when we place the stern of the boat to the wind. We have a lot of officers and soldiers going to fight in the Soudan — and no doubt they will see plenty of service. I have an officer of the Twenty-first Hussars as my companion.

I hope to receive news from you at Almeria. Writing Sunday, I should receive your letter Friday. Letters from home as you are aware are always very welcome. I must conclude. Kindly love to all, your affectionate husband

Thomas Morel'

In the second letter he expresses his view on a good wife. Of his wife's aunt he writes:

'She had been a good companion to the old boy and no doubt a good support and that seems to my mind the sum and total of married life, a wife that will be a drag and annoyance to her husband is a frightful mistake.

I hope Tom [now 25] will remember this and I would suggest you would guide him in the choice of a wife.

As to Ralph [now 21], I quite agree with you. I have begged of you to see what should be done long ago. I have seen that he is wasting his time. He should be sent either to West Hartlepool or to a good engineering school to fit him for the higher grade of his profession. Think the matter over so that we may take a decision on my arrival.'

Thomas made his usual journey 'about 50 miles up the mountains' and on his return noted that 'my trip up the hills tired me very much and could not complete my business today'.

He wrote, as always, of how important the letters from his wife and Gladys were to him:

'I can assure you it's very important to receive your news; it's the only pleasure I have in this most troublesome time I have to pass in this country.'

On his second trip to Andalusia in 1902 his son John, now aged nineteen, sailed on the SS *Gwentland* with the intention of joining his father some way through his stay there.

Thomas wrote to Susanna:

'at sea two hours off Gib, . . . We have had a splendid passage — the usual big rolling waves in the Bay. I shall expect a letter from you all on Thursday at Almeria. I forgot to instruct the office to send you cash for wages. Get Tom to bring it to you. All wages at the Lindens paid, a week due at St. Andrews.'

In the next letter he wrote from the Hotel Reine Christina at Algerciras:

'You will I am sure regret to know that I have caught a fearful cold — in fact I have never had such a dose . . . I am very feverish and quite blocked up, swollen in my nose and throat . . . and now I have quite collapsed.

I shall see a doctor tomorrow morning at Gib — I am not sure if it is safe for me to proceed. If I am in for a severe illness you will have to come here to nurse me. The *Gwentland* is not in sight at 5.30. I give her up until tomorrow . . . I have been anxious about John — that has added to my trouble. Your affectionate husband,

Thomas Morel'

Thomas Morel in the Gergal mountains in Southern Spain. Circa 1890.

However on the next day Saturday, 22nd February, he was able to write:

> 'You will be glad to know that the Dr. considers that I can safely proceed. The *Gwentland* passed St. Vincent at noon yesterday. She will be here in an hour or, latest, two. I will proceed at once.
>
> I have been very anxious about John picturing all sorts of harm that might happen — when you are not well you magnify these matters.'

He wrote the next letter from Estacronda, Gergal, on The Gergal Railway and Mines Company writing paper on 9th March, 1902:

> 'Your letter from Bournmouth to hand. Glad to see you are all pretty well — but you seem not very bright — Tom should not worry although no doubt it's his nature to do so. We are both well and working hard. We are staying in a house that belongs to me — a young engineer and his wife live there — they are very respectable and the wife is very bright. The house has been well done up and we feel pretty well. She (the wife) cooks with the help of a servant.
>
> We had a splendid day yesterday in the saddle for fully six hours up and down the mountain, a new experience for John, he stood it very well — today Sunday we are keeping as quiet as we can. I think the wife of Mr. Kitchen is a Methodist by the tunes I have heard her sing — I shall finish here Wed. pass the rest of the week at Almeria.'

Before leaving for home he wrote again from Gergal:

> 'I have no letter from you. No doubt letters are at Almeria. I shall be there D.V. tonight. We have had splendid weather a lot of sun — cool in fact perfect weather. As usual I have overtired myself. John did not go so far.'

His last letter of the trip is written from Almeria on 12th March:

> 'I have written you very often nearly every day. I try to get John to write also. I have a message from the S.S. *Barry*: if she can sail from Aguilas on Monday morning we might be at Gib on Wednesday we should be home Saturday.
>
> Glad to see Gladys is better. I was overtired yesterday I am therefore out of sorts today. I hope a couple of days will see me right again. I have before me 4/5 days of hard work to complete my business here. John is well and sends love and will write to you tomorrow . . . I am very tired of this place with all its petty questions and jealousies.'

His third visit to Almeria was made the following year in January 1903. He planned to sail on from Gibraltar on one of his own ships, the SS *Westergate*, but she was detained. He wrote to his daughter, Gladys, from the Hotel Reine Christina at Algerciras:

> '. . . you have to be careful and do not get your throat irritated, the remedy rests with you. We had a very bad passage — the wind changed against us and when we arrived yesterday it blew a gale from the East. We started with a S.W. strong wind; some ladies did not show themselves at table the whole time of the trip — I am not well myself but I attribute it to my old complaint. I am better since yesterday thanks to a good supply of warm water — still I am reminded that I am not well after each meal. This is a very fine place quite full. I had no end of difficulty to get in — Hotels are all full. If Uncle Philip and Aunt Mattie have not started for

Cannes tell them to secure their rooms before they start. I understand the Riviera is quite full. The weather today is splendid. I have been walking and sitting in the sunshine all day. The *Westergate* is I fear detained by weather. I have not yet had a telegram that she has arrived — this is vexing as I expect I shall have to vacate my room tomorrow. I shall try not to. I shall say; J'y suis, j'y reste.

Your loving father
Thomas Morel'

The second letter of this visit was sent to his wife from Almeria five days later, the *Westergate* having eventually reached Gibraltar.

'I found Almeria full of sunshine but high wind yesterday. I am better since I landed here — or say since I left Gib — trust this will continue — I trust you are keeping well — do not fret about the boys. They must behave and take care of you instead of being a burden.

I find Almeria improved and I think business has also taken a right turn.'

Thomas Morel's illness to which he referred in his letter to his daughter caused him two months later to go to Bournemouth to see his doctor. He went alone and stayed at the Royal Bath Hotel.

'Dr. Smith confirms what they all say, nervous dyspepsia — brought on by worry — he thinks it's not so bad as when he last saw me — recommends absolute rest and free of worry. This hotel is a very old stuffy place, the weather being fine I think I shall proceed on to Jersey — if you or Gladys care to come I shall be glad of your company.'

Gladys agreed to join him and he arranged to meet her at Weymouth. He asked to have his cloak brought and ten pounds in notes:...

'I am, thankful to say, better. I do not feel this dreadful sinking sickness — but I have still a touch of it nearly every meal. Gladys should take without fail her riding habit.'

It is suggested to him that John should come with Gladys:...

'Re John, I think he should wait another occasion — I had rather a bad time when we all three went to Russia — you must remember I am trying to have a rest. I cannot be burdened with the care of a number of the family. I am as you know rather prone to worry about things, the least thing puts me out.'

Thomas then proceeded to worry about his two properties:

'... You will have no doubt engaged a gardener – and his wife – Collins should be instructed to see what he can do to repair the corner of the dining room paper — we have some pieces of this paper upstairs in the closet — near Clem's room — also the morning room paper and ceiling should be touched up, also the W.C. paper renewed or partly so — but I don't want him to make a big job of this trifling work; they are all very fond of this ... The St. Andrews house should be got ready for our going in residence about the 8th or the 10th May. This I hope will suit you. ...'

In Jersey, Thomas and his daughter Gladys stayed at the Somerville Hotel, St. Aubin, and he wrote to his wife on 20th April:

'We have enjoyed our stay here very much. Gladys has been a very good companion and she has enjoyed herself being very interested in the Island and its inhabitants.'

Two months later, and for the last time, Thomas Morel went abroad again from 25th June to 15th July to try to find a cure for his illness at Vichy. He went alone.

His letters written to his wife and daughter have a real poignancy. His loneliness in this fashionable watering place is very marked and he does not spare his family at home the details of his illness. On the way, Thomas stayed in Paris and he wrote to his daughter:

> '. . . the country was very fine, fields of corn full of poppies and blue cornflowers — lots of acacias in full bloom on both sides of the road. . . . Paris was quite clean and fresh. I stayed at a very quiet hotel. . . . I went for two hours to the Salon Exhibition of pictures, very fine.
>
> You will want to know how I am. Just middling. I have not been sick for three days but not free from pain . . . I have not yet seen the doctor but they all say the cure lasts 21 days – if I have to stay you will have to come and keep me company.'

In the second letter and those following he wrote about Vichy:

> 'The description of this place is not very easy — it's a huge promenade — with a half a mile of covered way enabling visitors to walk about free from either rain or sun. Lots of trees in the parks, which are beautifully laid out, regardless of expense — the bathing establishment is a large place covering several acres — it's quite new, only opened some two months ago — and fitted out according to the new principle of hygene. I expect it's the best in Europe. We have a Casino — concerts are held every night and often in the afternoon. We have a splendid orchestra, the best I expect in Europe. It's a great treat to hear them play — a large theatre is also attached to it. Papers, both English, Spanish and, of course, French — also all the requirements of a first class club are here. I am sorry to say lots of people play at the gaming tables, — plenty of shops, but what is more interesting are the drinking places — there are no less than 10/12 springs of water — patients are sent by the doctors to a special spring according to their ailments. The first thing you do is to chose a doctor and you have to consult him every 3 days; he takes note of the effect of water on your system. I think I have pretty well described the plan.
>
> At the hotel, they serve three kinds of menues, an ordinary dinner for people who are well — a number of people come here for pleasure or what they call pleasure — play — say about 50% of those present — secondly, those suffering from diabetes — they must have special bread, no sugar and no fruit. Thirdly, I join the ranks of the dyspeptics — allowed bread, vegetables, sugar, some fruit, otherwise same as the diabetic menu, it's rather amusing. I go to bed at 9—9.30. Yesterday I went to my room at 8.30. I fear I am getting quite a hermit. . . . I continue my special baths every morning and my drinking the waters. Yesterday I had fifteen minutes massage sous l'eau, afterwards a friction with eau de Cologne. Today Vapor bath for twenty minutes, then douche, rest and another friction. I hope it will do me good, so far I do not see much change. It's a lot of trouble, but I hope it will result satisfactorily. . . . Here the weather is very hot, too hot, 80° in the shade, but they say it is the kind of weather to suit Vichy and

the Cure. No one goes out from 12 noon to 3 but I think it suits those like myself who have to take the waters and take hot baths.'

Later he wrote:

'. . . Yesterday the doctor did not find me so well, he reduced the quantity of water and stopped massage and douches. The fact is I missed the Bicarbonate of Soda — which for the last three to four months kept me free from pain or nearly free when I took it regularly — the Doctor here says these waters contain the element found in Carbonate of Soda but in a form that will cure; they are called by him 'living waters'. As you say I want rest from worry. I have had enough and to spare. Give all the letters that arrive for me to John who will instruct Johnson to open them and to say to the Sec. or others who call meetings that I am away — as there will be cash coming in from the end of the month Tom, will be able to endorse the cheques and deposit some at the bank. . . .'

He wrote to Susanna:

'I am pretty well. I think this place will do me good — the difficulty is the time it takes. I hope I shall have the patience to go through with it. I have had to give up my after meal coffee, cognac and even wine except very watered. The doctor explained that my stomach resembled a sour sore and when it collapsed the pain is caused by the two sides of the stomach coming together and is felt when the food has been digested — it's not a nice thing to write about it's not I assure you a nice thing to feel. Hence my hope in these waters is now centred in their curative powers. . . . When you write say how things are at Llansannor [Ed: Llansannor was an estate Thomas Morel owned in the Vale of Glamorgan.] and if you are hay harvesting . . . the meadows I suppose will all be done — re the Parsons meadow, I am not sure if I paid him . . .'

On the three Sundays that he was at Vichy he went to the French services. On 5th July:

'This is the third Sunday I shall have been away from home. Today we had long metre tunes. I had not heard them for thirtyfive years and they came quite familiar and I was able to join in the singing. We had a very good sermon on Christian politeness [sic] taking as his text Charity — it's quite strange and it reminded me of my boyhood to have the French liturgy.'

He heard regularly from his wife and Gladys, who described her nephew Ted. Thomas wrote about his grandson:

'you must have a good time with Teddy. Kiss him for me, he is a little darling and will be coming more and more a treasure. I think I am getting better. I have less pain and have not been sick since a week — this is saying a great deal.'

But on 9th July he had to write:

'. . . you will regret to hear I have had a serious set back; after the great heat we have had a change of weather and I must have caught a chill — this is what the doctor says. I was sick the day before yesterday — and yesterday — with feverish bad nights — it's a pity I had built up so much hope in this cure. I had, I fear, too severe a douche two days ago. The doctor has dropped these off for today and tomorrow. As I shall not stay in London by reason of the Cardiff Railway meeting being only on the 31st, on leaving Paris I shall travel right home.'

And finally on 15th July, beginning as he often did:

'I expected a letter from you this morning',

he continued:

I am writing you for the last time on this trip. I trust you are all well. For myself I do not feel much better still this sickness and pain every evening and night — but they all say I shall see the benefit from the treatment and waters when I get home — I hope so.

I felt longing to come home today. I don't see what is the magic in the number 21 [ed. the length of the cure] but everyone obeys the order. Yesterday was celebrated the National fete — quite a commotion.

I will write from Paddington for the time Vokings [Ed. his coachman] must meet me at Dinas Powis. With love to you all. Your affectionate husband, Thomas Morel.'

Thomas Morel died on 7th October, 1903 three months after returning home; he was 56 years of age. As his letters show, he had long suffered from gastric disorders and at the end these stomach ulcers became malignant. Again and again he was given the impractical advice 'not to worry'. His actual death was due to heart failure.

His death, funeral and the details of his will were fully treated in the *Western Mail*, the *South Wales Daily News* and the *Evening Express* and reported in papers throughout the British Isles. From the South Wales papers:

'The mortal remains of the late Sir Thomas Morel were on Saturday afternoon laid to rest in the family vault at Cardiff Cemetery amidst many manifestations of sorrow and regret. Considering the important position which the deceased had occupied in the public life of the district and the large commercial interests with which he was connected in South Wales it was not surprising that there was a large and representative attendance not only from Cardiff and Penarth but from Newport and other parts of South Wales as well. Before leaving the residence of the deceased at Dinas Powis, a short service at which the members of the household were present was held at which the Rev. Robert Bond, minister of Trinity Wesleyan Church, Penarth of which the deceased was a member, read a passage of Scripture and offered prayer. The cortege, consisting of the hearse and nine mourning coaches containing the chief mourners left St. Andrews' House, Dinas Powis, shortly before 1 o'clock. Following the coffin which was borne in an open car came the deceased's private carriage.

The Cortege reached Grangetown about half past one o'clock. In accordance with arrangements most of those who were attending the funeral were waiting at Clive Street, Grangetown. The Chief Constable with mounted police headed the procession and after there came a carriage containing Dr. Cook and Dr. Fred Evans (Medical Advisors). The Rev. Robert Bond and Mr. Donald Maclean (Solicitor). Then followed in carriages the Mayor of Cardiff in his robes and chain of office while the Mace-bearers riding on box seats carried their Maces draped in crepe followed by the members of the Corporation. In the first carriage with his Worship rode the Mayor of Newport, the ex-Mayor of Cardiff and the Town Clerk

> and the procession was made up of over 50 carriages. Large crowds lined the streets and most men took off their hats as the hearse passed along them. Many of the licensed houses along the route closed their doors for a brief period and the blinds at all the principal places of business in the town were drawn. At the Town Hall a number of the borough police force was drawn up in line. There was also a section of the Bute Docks police. At the cemetery a large number of people had assembled but as the vault was roped in they did not interfere in the slightest with the last sad rite. In the small Nonconformist Chapel the Rev. Robert Bond read the burial service prescribed for those of the Wesleyan faith and he also officiated at the graveside. The walls of the family vault were lined with moss and white chrysanthemums. At the conclusion of the Service the Choir of Trinity Church, Penarth led those present in singing the hymn, Rock of Ages.
>
> Sir William Thomas Lewis, Bart. was present as Lord Bute's representative. Sir William came specially from Pembrokeshire to pay a last tribute to the memory of Sir Thomas who was greatly respected both by the present marquis and his lordship's late father, who was ever prepared to recognise that Sir Thomas had done a great deal for the import trade of Cardiff, as well as for the export trade.'

Sir Thomas Morel left £304,670.9.5d. gross, £283,190.11.1d. net and death duties were paid at £19,880.

In his will, Thomas Morel left his widow all his household effects and £2,000 a year for her lifetime and the choice of living in either of his two houses, The Lindens or St. Andrews House. These, incidentally, were leasehold and together with his half share of 2 Stuart Street, were valued at £4,075 in all.

He had life insurance policies of £19,010 and his Llansannor estate in the Vale of Glamorgan was valued at £8,352. His ownership of this estate gave him the right, despite his Methodism, to appoint to the living of Llansannor. During his wife's lifetime, the balance of the income from his estate was to be divided equally between his four sons and his daughter. After Susanna Morel's death the estate was to pass to the five in equal shares absolutely, except for the power reserved to the Trustees, of whom the only one would have been Tom, on his mother's death, of postponing payment to any of his children, 'until such a time as they thought fit'.

In a codecil, the Trustees were given the fullest power of postponing the realization of all or part of the estate for as long as they thought fit. This was clearly to avoid the situation which faced the executors on the death of John Angel Gibbs, whose will gave no such latitude, so that they were forced to call in all the holdings in Morel Limited with such traumatic consequences.

The will and further codecil expressly confirmed Tom 'to act and assist at a salary in the management in the place of his father in the Firm of Morel Brothers and Co' and declared that Tom 'shall receive for his own benefit the testators own half share of the profits of Morel Brothers and Co, namely one half of £2,000 per annum and one half of the 5% on the net profit of Morel Ltd.'

After Tom's death the next surviving son was to take his place.

Thomas Morel's holding in Morel Limited was valued for Estate Duty purposes at £60,576.10.0d. which was less than a quarter of the £250,000 at which it stood at the incorporation of Morel Limited in 1884. Being in a private company the shares were not freely negotiable and it was their estimated market value rather than any exact valuation of Thomas's holdings in the ships, that would have been the agreed basis for this evaluation.

Apart from establishing Tom's place in the Firm, the will shows something of the Jersey pattern; all the sons inherited equally and the daughter, Gladys, was brought in on similar terms.

CHAPTER EIGHT

1903-1919

The death of Thomas Morel, the removal of his influence, and the consequent release of large sums of money to each of his children affected them profoundly in different ways. No longer were they beholden to him for advancement or subject to his financial control. Tom the eldest, always responsible and already in Morel Limited, assumed his father's place in the Firm. He had married Edith Moxey in 1899, and they lived in Penarth at 3 Park Road and later in Roxburgh, a large red brick house opposite the Railway Station. Her family were coal agents and had coaling stations at ports around the world. Tom was a pillar of the Wesleyan Church, the superintendent of the very large Sunday School at Trinity and an occupier of the back pew in the Church, an indication of his assured leadership there. His wife and her family, too, were Wesleyans. He enjoyed riding and there were always enough horses in the St. Andrews House stables to provide a mount for any member of the family. Whilst he was not uninterested in racing form and odds, he resolutely refused to gamble on racehorses — nor indeed did he drink, being a loyal and convinced believer in his Church's social witness of that period.

His son, Ted (Thomas Edwin) was born in 1903, but shortly after his birth Edith, his mother, became mentally ill and remained of unsound mind until her death twenty years later. Tom made it possible for his wife to remain in her home in Penarth. She had a nurse and a companion and her own suite of rooms in a wing especially added to the house. These provisions did not cripple him financially, but his social life was grievously affected and it underlined his different pattern of life from his brothers, who were branching out in other directions.

Less than a month before his father's death, Ralph, the second of Sir Thomas's sons, when he was 26, married Amy, the eldest daughter of John Cory and grand-daughter of Thomas and Philip's contemporary, the elder John Cory.

John Cory, the founder of John Cory and Sons, had retired to Newport and his elder son, John, had moved to Sea View, Penarth. The Thomas Morel and John Cory families visited each other frequently, their Penarth houses being only a short distance apart. There was one slight differentiating factor; although both families were Wesleyans, the Corys identified themselves with the older chapel in Penarth whereas the Morels were amongst those who pioneered the move of the new cause, Trinity, to a rural site, Woodland Place, on the outskirts of the town. Probably neither the Corys nor the Morels wanted to live too much in the shadow of the other family; they were already rivals in

The wedding of Ralph Morel and Amy Cory in 1903. The best man is Clem Morel and the bridesmaids, from left to right, are Florence Cory, Gladys Morel, Brenda Cory and Susan Gibbs. The flower girl is Marjorie Cory.

the commercial life of Cardiff Docks, and a little distancing in their church life did not come amiss.

Ralph and Amy, after a short time in Penarth, moved to St. Andrews House on his father's death, as Susanna had chosen to live in The Lindens in her widowhood. Ralph had trained in marine engineering in the North of England and brought this specialized knowledge to the Firm. It was not unusual for him to return to 2 Stuart Street almost unrecognisable in his working clothes from inspecting the boilers of one of the Morel ships berthed at Cardiff Docks. On his father's death, he inherited enough capital to enable him to become a shipowner on his own account as R.E. Morel and Co. and at one time he owned as many as four ships.

Ralph Morel rode to hounds as did a number of docksmen, and horses played a prominent part in his life both for hunting and racing. He also played polo and hockey at the Whitchurch Club often taking his young relative, and office boy, Clem Scriven, out of the office to play hockey with him. A kind and popular man, he was to acquire during the period of his war service in Africa the habit of hard drinking which was to remain with him all his life. His church

The four Morel brothers on the steps of the Lindens, on the day of their sister Gladys's wedding, April 21 1909. From left to right Tom, Clem, Ralph, John.

allegiance was to become nominal but his Methodist heritage was strong enough to cause him to insist that his daughter should be married at Trinity Methodist Church, howbeit 'secretly' and contrary to her choice in the matter.

Clem, the third son, caused his parents considerable distress. He was possessed of very great charm — it was said that 'a dance with Clem made any girl's evening'. His father was anxious that he should acquire a legal qualification — a solicitor in the Firm would have been very valuable.

He went to a Law-crammers in London, and for a time his sister, Gladys, was sent there by her parents to keep house and to be a sobering influence upon him. When in Vichy just before his death, Thomas had written sadly in a letter to his wife:

> 'This morning I studied the list of those who passed their exams. I did not find Clem's name. I did not expect to find his name. It's very sad . . .'

Thomas's death was the release for which Clem was waiting. He went to Ireland, where he was able to hunt six days a week and rest on Sundays. He saw the chance of becoming 'Master of the Tips' — the Tipperary Hounds, and decided that he must have a wife who could sit a horse in a manner fitting for the wife of a Master of the Fox Hounds. After some hesitation, for he had been visiting Brenda Cory, Amy's sister, frequently, he took himself off to Gloucestershire and married Gladys Masters who sat a horse beautifully. They went to live in Ireland at Tullamaine Castle in Tipperary which, later, was burnt down in one of the Sinn Fein risings.

John, the youngest son, was twenty when his father died. With three older brothers he was obsessed with the need to hold his own. He accompanied his older brother, Clem, to South Africa on a big game hunting safari; it seems that before his marriage Clem had needed to be rescued from what was considered at the time to be an unsuitable entanglement and shooting big game was one of the accepted methods of providing distraction.

John brought back a fine collection of heads and horns which were on display in his home for many years. When asked by a great nephew, in an age in which the camera was increasingly taking over from the gun, whether shooting such fine animals caused him any distress at the time, he brushed the question aside, 'No, I was only determined to hold my own and shoot as many as my brother did'.

This remained John Morel's problem and his spur all his business life, and in his social life as well. In almost everything he wanted to do he was frustrated because there were few courses of action he could originate.

This, however, did not prevent his marrying Brenda Cory; thus repeating in his generation the same pattern that Philip and Thomas had set in theirs — the marrying of two sisters by two brothers.

Gladys, very much the darling of her father, regarded herself as something of a tomboy, growing up as she did with four brothers. She rode, enjoyed the farm, and also helped her mother run the Women's Hour at the Church. It was clearly going to be difficult for anyone to marry her. She was an heiress and her brothers teased her, saying that in her father's eyes 'only a religious earl would have been good enough for her'. Her father's death was to be a release for her also.

She spent much time with 'the No. 5 Friends', both with the girls and the boys, and she and the young John Angel Gibbs, who had been at school with her brother Ralph, fell in love. They had to meet secretly — by the bridge in the Windsor Gardens (since demolished) as her family would not countenance her marrying a Gibbs, with only the prospects of a junior clerk to boot.

For her mother, the question of marriage with a cousin did not pose any particular problem — marriage between cousins was a common practice on Portland — but even when her father was dead Gladys had her brothers' opposition to break down.

She was often very unhappy and her mother was quite unable to protect her from the persecution she suffered from some of her brothers who felt John Angel's comparative impecuniosity to be an affront.

In March 1906 Gladys joined Tom and his wife, Edith, on a visit to Egypt. This would seem to have been a ploy to distract her from the resolve to marry her cousin.

Susanna wrote to her daughter:

> '. . . I was quite unprepared to see you so broken down. I am sure you might have thought me very unsympathetic, only, dear, you know all my love for you and sometimes I feel so helpless . . . you must not think yourself unloved, for there are many, many who love you much. Sarah and I go on just the same after you left'.

It was not until three years later that Gladys and John Angel Gibbs did marry. Her brothers' opposition to the match was eventually worn down, helped by John Angel Gibbs's success as a shipowner in his own right. He, of all his brothers, inherited his father's flair and ability. In 1905, he convinced the manager of the Midland Bank at Cardiff Docks that he knew enough about ships and ship management to be granted a loan. He had been with the shipping firm of Pyman, Watson and Company in Cardiff for some years after working in London with the London and Provincial Bank. It was helpful, too, that he bore the name of his father, John Angel Gibbs, whose reputation as a partner in Morel Brothers and Company would still have been remembered at Cardiff Docks. He would have had to admit, if pressed, that his father died when he was four years old and he had not been able to pick up any shipping lore around the family dining table. However, in 1906 when he was 26 years old he founded the South Wales Steamship Company and was joined in 1909 by his elder brother, William, who returned from London, having also learned the business of ship broking in the London Office of Pyman Brothers.

Gibbs and Company managed their ships by the usual single ship Company method. Their first steamer was the *SS South Wales* of 3,668 gross tons and she was soon employed in the traditional tramp routine of 'coal outward, grain inward', largely with Rio de Janeiro and other South American ports. The business prospered, so two further steamers were ordered and by 1915 their fleet consisted of three ships.

There was no question of a partnership between the Morels and the young Gibbs. The two families managed their ships at a distance from each other. The Morels had fifty years experience behind them and very large resources in their Firm and in their personal fortunes. The Gibbs had, at first, almost no financial resources but they had a keen ambition to make up for the years when, through their father's early death, they had had no stake in shipping.

Gladys's brothers could not sustain their opposition to her marriage with a rising young docksman and she and John Angel Gibbs were married at Trinity on 21st April, 1909.

Another person who was no friend to the early love of Gladys and John was Sarah Scriven, briefly mentioned in Susanna's letter to her daughter. According to her nephew, Clem Scriven, she was not above reporting on their unofficial meetings. Sarah, a Portlander, was a niece of Elizabeth Gibbs and companion to Susanna Morel.

The women of the family expected to be supported by other women, especially when they were widowed or their daughters had left home. When a daughter went on holiday, a female relation would take her place even for a short period.

The role of companion provided unmarried women of very limited means with a standard of living to which they could not aspire on their own. Martha Morel had 'her' Miss Wake and Robert Gibbs's widow 'her' Miss Vickers and Lady Morel 'her' Sarah Scriven. The role was an equivocal one which gave no certainty of a livelihood when the one they companioned came to die. Inevitably their attitude to their employers had a sycophantic ring: 'Mrs Morel has decided' . . . 'Mrs. Gibbs says . . .'. Listening to them, it was difficult not to be persuaded that those to whom they were companions were possessed of a vast amount of commonsense and a flashing wit.

After marriage, a daughter was expected to visit her mother regularly, even daily, and family letters of the period are full of references to morning and afternoon calls, notwithstanding that the callers, this time with their husbands, might be expected to come to the house again for dinner in the evening.

Susanna Angel Gibbs returned from Portland to a house in Dumfries Place, Cardiff, after the death of her husband, William, in 1870, with her unmarried daughter Ann. Her daughter Susanna Morel, often accompanied by her own daughter Gladys, visited her almost every day driving over from Penarth by carriage. Gladys remembered that there were often several family carriages outside her grandmother's house, and that when Susanna Angel Gibbs returned the visits she carried with her a cap in a small box to wear inside the house when she removed her bonnet.

Susanna Morel expected the same attention from her daughter on her marriage. Even when newly married Gladys had to leave her new house, No. 3 Park Road, which she and her husband had taken over from the Tom Morels, and spend either the morning or the afternoon sitting with her mother at The Lindens.

A mother did not expect the same attention or support from her sons. In her widowhood, Susanna could do little but plead with them: '. . . I desire the best things for you but to have them we must set our faces towards them'. In a letter to her youngest son, John, who had gone to Ireland to stay with Clem, she wrote, without enthusiasm, about point to point races and hunting: 'The country will be strange to you so take care if you have a day's hunting.' Then, obliquely, by way of example: 'I went to Church this morning — Mr. Bond was better than usual — Ralph and Amy were out this morning [in church] and have paid us a little visit this afternoon.'

During Thomas's lifetime Susanna had supported her husband in his public career. Her obituary later said of her:

> 'She was Mayoress of Cardiff in 1898 and in that year greatly assisted her late husband in his onerous duties as Chief Magistrate.'

She was not, however, at ease in her public role and after her husband's death was happy to concentrate upon her chapel and her family. In addition to the Sunday services she was a regular attender at the weekly Class Meetings at Trinity — indeed a staunch Wesleyan.

Christine Nance wrote to the author from her personal experience:

> 'Susanna was not made for public life. Sir Thomas enjoyed his position especially as Mayor of Cardiff, but Mrs. Morel hated publicity and would look quite miserable when she had to appear in public on a platform. She enjoyed her quiet family life with her husband and children. Her greatest happiness had been when they were first married. In later life she was very sad and told me that her husband had changed entirely since their early married life.'

However much she hated travelling abroad, it is strange that at least she did not accompany Thomas on his last trip to Vichy — or arrange for Gladys to go with him.

Her family interest had never been limited to her own immediate family. As the nineteenth century passed more and more Portland names were heard in Cardiff and Penarth such as Angel, Scriven, Pearce and Hinde. The success of the Firm drew young men from the Island to Cardiff Docks and Susanna was able to influence the placing of her young relatives in the family Firm and in other firms connected with shipping. The claims of the extended family worked strongly through the distaff side. A chance conversation at afternoon tea at The Lindens or Penarth House or amongst the No. 5 friends might, for example, throw up the name of a young boy, William Hinde, who was of an age to start at the Docks and of a young Scriven girl, Annie, who might well come to live with her aunt at No. 5 for a few months. When these two did come to Penarth it is not surprising that they eventually married and increased the number of Portlanders who moved from the Isle with its limited opportunities to the thriving Docks at Cardiff. The Morel brothers were, however, not joined by any of their younger relatives from Jersey once the initial move in the 1850s and 60s had been made; providing for younger relatives was predominantly a female occupation. The Jersey connection was, however, maintained as some third of the captains of the Morel ships in the 1880s and again in the 1900s were Jerseymen.[1]

In her last years Susanna Morel was in poor health and had a nurse permanently living with her in addition to Sarah Scriven. Susanna died on a Sunday evening in October, 1910. 'The members of the family who were at home left early in the evening to attend Chapel. Soon afterwards Lady Morel had a heart seizure and realising that it was serious the nurse at once summoned the members of the family. Her daughter and others were attending service at Trinity and on receiving the message they at once left the Chapel. Lady Morel, however, had passed away before their arrival.'

In contrast to the effect on his family Thomas Morel's death did not overtly disturb the tenor of the Company. Indeed, no record of his death occurs in the minute book, which is consistent with the Company's usual practice; the minutes seldom included details of matters other than those required by law.

Whilst in the actual number of ships owned Morels may have still had the largest fleet in Cardiff in 1903, their average net tonnage was only 1380 tons and this in comparison with John Cory's average of 1658 net tons, Evan Thomas, Radcliffe of 1835 net tons, and W.T. Tatem and Co. of 2435 net tons. The age of their fleet and the policy of non-replacement they adopted after 1904 ensured that they would soon be overtaken by all these Companies, as proved to be the case in 1913. The decline in the strength and thrust of the Firm, which became apparent from 1903 onwards, cannot be attributed solely to Thomas Morel's death in 1903 as other factors were at work prior to this.

From 1899 onwards, Morel names other than that of the Morel Firm itself appeared in the Lloyds Register of Shipping. Philip Morel and his son, Willie, became owners of one ship each in that year and were joined by Willie's elder brother, Philip E. Morel, in 1901. The year 1902 saw the addition of Ralph Morel and Co. and by 1906 both he and Willie Morel owned four ships each. During the First World War, Ralph Morel's Company was the only individual one on the Register and he sold his two remaining ships to Morel Limited in 1921.

It was not uncommon for docksmen to own ships in their own right. Neither Ralph Morel nor Willie Morel were partners in Morel Brothers and Company, nor directors of Morel Limited and ownership of their own ships would have, to a degree, approximated their position financially to those of their elder brothers. At a time when Morel Limited was not building up its own fleet such activity, particularly on the part of Philip Morel and of his elder son, indicated a lack of cohesion and a dissipation of energy in contrast with the singleness of purpose of the early years of the Firm.

Such diversified activity can be illustrated by the history of SS *Nolisment,* which also gives some indication of the cost of vessels and their trading profitability in the 1900s.

In 1902, Philip Morel, on his own account, had built by Wm. Gray of West Hartlepool the *Nolisment* of 3828 tons dead weight, 2492 tons net, at a cost of £44,000 and he assigned the management of this ship to his son, Willie Morel, under the designation of W.G. Morel and Co., managers.

Two years later, Willie reported that the boat 'had been very successful having cleared £8,000 during the past two years'.

In 1909, he stated that in the previous year the profit on the ship had been £2,500; £2,000 of which had been distributed as dividend and £500 placed on reserve. In 1911 the *Nolisment* was sold for £23,000, a rate of depreciation that was not unusual, to Ralph Morel and Co. who continued to manage her for a year before they sold her to another Cardiff firm.

Morel Limited firmly maintained its private status. Following on the Companies Act of 1907 it was resolved that 'the number of members of the Company shall not at any time exceed fifty', and, more importantly, that 'no invitation shall be made by the Company to the public to subscribe for any share or debentures of the Company'. This clause confirmed Morel Limited's status as a private company within the control of the family.

From 1903 onwards the Company consistently declared a dividend of 2% carrying forward an average of some £4,000 each year but in 1908 the dividend was passed and even the Directors' Fees of £710 for 1907 and Directors and Rail Fees of £442 for 1908 were carried to the Special Reserve Account. Somewhat exceptionally, the amount standing to the profit and loss account for 1908 revealed: £20,344.17.6d.

In 1910 at a directors meeting:

> 'Letters were read from the London and Provincial Bank Limited and Lloyds Bank Limited regarding the debit balances of The Beignon Steamship Company Ltd., The Cyfarthfa Steamship Company Limited, The Dowlais Steamship Company Ltd. and The Portugalette Steamship Company Ltd. whose accounts are guaranteed by Morel Limited and calling upon these Companies to discharge their

liabilities to the said Banks.

In view of the impossibility of selling the steamers by a forced sale at the present time at anything like their value, it was decided to put the accounts in credit through the Insurance Funds, and it was agreed that should either of the Partners call in the money so advanced by the Insurance Funds the amount should be repaid within one month from the date of such notice, it being agreed that the liability on these accounts should be liquidated by Morel Limited.'

There was little recovery for three years, both for Morels and shipping in general.

In the middle of the slump in shipping, Philip Morel, the elder of the two Morel Brothers and the first Chairman of the Company, died on 2nd February, 1908. He was 67 and he survived his younger brother by five years. The minute book took no cognizance of the event save that his son, Philip, signed as chairman in his place.

His obituary in the Cardiff papers was noticeably shorter than that of his late brother, partly because there was no one to give accurate information about his early life, as he would have done in Thomas's case, and partly because there was less to write about him. It was noted that —

> 'He never took a very active part in public life. He was, however, a justice of the peace for the County of Glamorgan. He was a Wesleyan. His elder son, Philip E. Morel is a partner in Morel Ltd. and his second son, Willie G. Morel, is in business on his own account as a shipowner at Cardiff.'

Mr. Philip Morel's will was proved at £410,299.7.4d. gross, £355,232, nett. He left Martha, his wife, £2,000 a year and after that divided the income of his estate between his children. Eventually his estate was to be divided between his four children, two of whom were daughters, in equal shares, but the capital was held in trust for their respective children and it was, therefore, not a direct inheritance as it was in the case of his brother Thomas's children. He was perhaps fearful that his daughters might be wooed for their money and not for themselves, and that his sons might kick over the traces. The will followed closely that of his brother Thomas, having been drawn up by the same solicitor, Mr. Arthur Ingledew. He gave his trustees the fullest possible powers over the disposition of his estate with absolute discretion to postpone for any period a sale of his shares in ship or shipping companies or other property of a wasting nature — a clause inserted as with Thomas's will to relieve his executors of the predicament which faced the executors of John Angel Gibbs's estate. His son Philip was confirmed as his successor in the Firm of Morel Brothers and Co. under the identical terms with Tom E. Morel in his father's will. His estate was greater than that of his brother, who had died five years before, by some £127,000.

However, in 1903 the stock market had been depressed and the variation in the two estates may well be due to the fact that one will was proved when the stock market was low and the second five years later when it had recovered by possibly as much as 20%.

The policy of the Firm following Thomas Morel's death was one of almost complete retrenchment. Apart from having replacements built in 1904 for the SS *Dowlais* and the SS *Cyfarthfa* and from taking over one of Willie Morel's ships, the SS *Cardiff*, in 1911, they undertook no new ventures. Four of their ships were stranded or wrecked and of the others, fifteen were sold between 1904 and the outbreak of the War and six were sold between 1915 and 1916. The second *Dowlais* and the second *Cyfarthfa* which were all that remained of their fleet were both torpedoed and sunk within eight months of each other in 1917. Of the ships Morels had sold between 1904 and 1916, nine were torpedoed or mined.

The Morel and the Gibbs families were not spared the loss of life and the strain of living in wartime; thus the history of a family may encapsulate in its way the history of a country.

Ralph Morel enlisted in a cavalry regiment, served in North Africa, and was commissioned as a captain. The War was a searing experience for him. Clem Morel as a lieutenant was injured at Gallipoli but continued in the Army becoming a major by the end of the War. It was Gladys Morel, since 1909 Gladys Gibbs, however, on whom the War made its most lasting impact because her husband, John Angel Gibbs, was killed in 1917 whilst leading his Battalion in the attack on the Menin Road.

As head of a shipping company he had been under no compulsion to volunteer, but in the early days of the War he enlisted as a trooper in the Yeomanry and quickly became commissioned in the 9th Battalion Welch Regiment. He went to the front in February 1916, was early mentioned in despatches and was awarded a D.S.O.

John Angel Gibbs, who his Uncle William Benjamin on writing to Gladys Morel on her engagement described as 'the good boy of the Gibbs family', had been interested in 'work amongst lads' and within a few months of his death his widow bought the former Penarth Hotel as a Branch of the National Children's Home as a memorial to her late husband.

The house was to be used for the education and training of boys for the sea and engineering trades, preference being given to the needy sons of men who had fallen in the Welch Regiment. The first boys arrived in 1918.

John Angel Gibbs's death was a very grave blow to Gibbs and Company as he was founder and moving spirit of the Firm. He left his interest in the Management Company of the Firm to his two brothers, William and Reggie, the latter of whom after a spell in Cory Brothers had moved across to join Gibbs and Co. John was survived by his widow and five year-old son, John Morel Gibbs. By 1918, all three Gibbs ships had been lost by enemy action.

In 1912 shipping improved as the preparations for the First World War began to have their effect on freights. War and natural or man-made disasters, when food or goods have to be taken to a particular part of the world by a particular time, are reflected in soaring freights, especially if there is an overall shortage of world tonnage, and, although the minute book makes no reference to world events, their effect is reflected in the Firm's position from 1912 onwards. Morel Limited took advantage of this position to step up the sales of their ships rather than continue trading with them themselves.

Dividends at 4% were paid in 1913 rising to 10% in 1916 with sums of up to £20,000 carried forward.

After 1916 no dividend was declared and there was no indication at the annual general meetings of what sums were carried forward if any.

In November 1917, there was a family disagreement at the annual general meeting of Morel Limited which was recorded in the Minute Book.

> 'William G. Morel proposed that a dividend of 4% be declared but as this was not seconded, it was not put to the meeting.'

This is the first overt sign of a breach between the families. Philip E. had not attended any annual general meeting after 1915 and although the Directors did declare a dividend of 10% on 19th December — which would involve the paying out of £50,000 — a belated and disproportionate response to Willie's motion — there was clearly a crisis in the Firm. The Thirty fifth Annual Meeting in 1919 was attended by four members of the Philip Morel family; Martha and Maud making their first and only appearance. The minutes, apart from recording the appointment of Willie as a Director, reveal nothing, but the discussion amongst the members of the family when the formal business of the annual meeting was out of the way, must have revolved around how best to bring about the withdrawal from the Company of the interests of all the members of the late Philip Morel's family — which was what they wanted. Willie's appointment as a director would have been effected to make him eligible for compensation for loss of office along with his brother. Philip E. and Willie were in their late forties, wealthy men who felt the time had come to follow country pursuits. The War was over and they did not relish the prospect of continuing in business indefinitely side by side with their cousins. They had decided to get out of shipping.

At a directors' meeting on 2nd July, 1919 it was reported that 'by a Deed entered into this day Philip E. Morel and William G. Morel cease to be members of the Firm of Morel Brothers and Company and Directors of Morel Limited and that by a further deed entered into this day Ralph Elliot Morel of Saint Andrews, Dinas Powis and John Gibbs Morel of Henstaff Court in the County of Glamorgan having become members of the Firm of Morel Brothers and Company they are hereby appointed Directors of Morel Limited in place of the said Philip E. Morel and William G. Morel resigned, and it was resolved that they are hereby authorised to undertake the management of Morel Limited'.

The policy of Morel Limited since 1903 had been one of realization of assets and resting on its former achievements. As we have seen by 1918, there were no ships left to manage and the Morels were shipowners in name only.

Philip E. Morel had married Janet Salisbury, the eldest daughter of the Rector of Tredunnock, near Usk. The Salisburys were an old Denbighshire family of Norman descent. Philip E. and Janet lived first in the lodge of Batholey Park, the house itself having been destroyed by fire, and later at Glen Court, Usk.

It is puzzling to see how, living at this distance, he could take a very active part in the day to day running of the Firm. Even at annual general meetings he was frequently absent.

He was now to move much further away — to the Erines, a Victorian castle near Tarbert, Argyllshire, with his three daughters, Ursula, who married a professional soldier, Sylvia and Barbara. Here he was able to indulge his tendency to withdrawal to the full, living the life of a Scottish laird with some farming and sea fishing and surrounding himself with fine books. He died there at the age of 78.

Willie Morel had married Edith Jacks of Bristol. Her father was a draper who worked in Jones's in Bristol, which he later owned. She had aspirations to a larger life than was possible living in Rogermoor House in Victoria Road, in Penarth. In 1918 she was thirty-three. She influenced her husband to move first to Clifton and then to Bicknall Manor, Timberscombe in Somerset. He had no compunction about retiring from business at 40 and moving away from Penarth. He always maintained that he had worked very hard and doubted whether he would live long on retirement. In the event, he lived until his seventy-ninth year.

He enjoyed the life of a Somerset squire and he fitted the part well, but it was Edith who took wings, hunting with the Devon and Somerset Staghounds — she was a superb horsewoman — and driving fast cars, principally Napiers, becoming the first woman member of the Royal Automobile Club. For eleven years she lived in Sherborne and hunted with the Blackmore Vale, returning to Bicknall only 'when the oats ran out' as she put it, in the Second World War.

They had four children; Mervyn became a Surgeon, Bettina, a barrister, Wendy went to the Slade School of Art, and Yvonne became an engineer.

Not infrequently the suggestion is made that to become accepted into County society it is necessary to marry into it. This did not seem to be the case with the Philip Morels in Scotland or Somerset, or the Thomas Morels in Glamorgan or Tipperary. Enough money to buy a property and to maintain it, and, above all, an ability to ride, if possible, well, opened all doors.

As to the manner born, Willie Morel walked around the Bicknall Estate with his gun under his arm and, as president, greeted the members of the old Timberscombe Friendly Society with their decorated staves on their Club Day, offering them the hospitality of his house.

From 1919 onwards, with Philip E. and Willie's departure, the control of what remained of the Firm was concentrated, in the family of Thomas Morel, namely, his four sons and one daughter with A.R. Chenhalls as manager. They proceeded cautiously to build it up once more, but never to its former eminence.

CHAPTER NINE

Tom Morel's Chairmanship 1919-1935

> 'You can always judge the prosperity of a city or a country by the number of its millionaires. The more millionaires the more prosperity. Just after the last war Cardiff had more than twenty millionaires, though one or two of them may have been a bit speculative.' *Western Mail*

In 1919, of the Directors of Morel Limited Ralph Morel's status might have been 'a bit speculative' as he spent heavily in furtherance of his sporting interests particularly boxing, hunting and greyhound racing. He was a friend of Jimmy Wilde and also of Jack Peterson who trained for many of his fights at St. Andrews. He was a prominent director of Chepstow Racecourse. It is probable that the writer would have counted Tom and John Morel as amongst the 'non-speculative' millionaires, although their patterns of living in no way revealed their millionaire status and reflected nothing of the heady prosperity surrounding them.

Misquoting James Thomson's 'The City of Dreadful Night', Cardiff became known in the '20s as 'The City of Dreadful Knights' as a result of Lloyd George's policy of creating titles in response to donations to Liberal Party funds. Men who, it was said, 'didn't know one end of a ship from the other' borrowed money from their banks and bought ships at grossly inflated prices. 'Although the business was of a risky character, the banks did not seem to regard it with disfavour and the various flotations were generously financed, in some cases up to two-thirds of the abnormally high costs.'[1] The new shipowners revelled in the good life, patronizing the older shipowners such as the Corys and the Morels as well as the later docksmen of the 1890s. They gave lavish parties, even for children, giving take-home presents such as a small billiard table. They pressed ahead flaunting their quickly won wealth, blithely guaranteeing each others overdrafts. When the depression hit in 1920 and they were required to honour these personal guarantees they were unable to do so and they crashed together bringing each other down, not a few taking their own lives when faced with bankruptcy.

In the Firm, Tom Morel's style of chairmanship, reflecting the character of the man, enabled Morel Limited to rebuild gradually throughout this period in an unspectacular and responsible manner. A 'Who is it?' profile of this period in the *Western Mail* described him:

> 'A somewhat little man with a strong face and prominent features, and a continuous wearer of spectacles, he is the possessor of a remarkably quick mind and has the habit of quite definite expressions of opinion. A very able son of an able father.
>
> He has had a life experience of shipping, and is the present owner of many

ships. There is nothing in connection with the industry with which he is not conversant, and he is the wise counsellor of many of the younger generation.

Quiet, unostentatious, he is the strong man when required, and has a grip of detail which often stands him in good stead. A strong supporter of a certain religious cause he is the force in works of charity connected therewith.

He can be claimed as a foremost authority on shipping, and a pillar in the commercial structure of Cardiff Docks. There is an old English proverb which says "Money makes the man". [sic] With regard to the subject of this note I think the French version "Les Affaires font les hommes" more strictly applies.'

In 1919 and 1920, the years of great prosperity, Morel Limited had no ships at all and it was only in 1921 that they acquired two of the ships owned personally by Ralph Morel, the SS *Nolisment* and the SS *St. Andrews*. They bought two further ships, which had been built pre-war, in 1923, and it was not until 1925 that they ordered new ships on their own account. They did not, in consequence, have to meet the slump of 1920 onwards when freight dropped by between 50% and 300%. It was as if they gained real satisfaction from pursuing a policy in direct opposition to those around them.

Nor did the dividend policy for the period of Tom Morel's chairmanship reflect that of British shipping firms generally. Between 1920 and 1935 not once did they declare a higher dividend than 2½% and for eleven years the dividend was either 1% or passed.

As Morel Limited had no ships trading in 1919 or 1920 it is clear that their dividends of 2½% and 2% must have been paid out of capital reserves. Unlike the new men, who could not believe that the boom would ever end, the Morels had seen good days and bad days before and the Directors were aware of the danger of depending on any one industry — of having eggs only in one basket. As if to underline their policy of creating a strong capital position, at their directors meeting in 1924 they passed the resolution:

'At all times no less than £250,000 of the investments of Morel Limited must be in securities other than steamships of Steamship Companies.'

In 1926 the Firm presented Thomas Morel with a silver salver. Inscribed on it were the names of the staff of Morel Brothers and Co. at the time: Charles J. Hill in the London Office, Secretary, William H. Johnson. Manager, W. Rutter. Engineer, Tom Fox with A. Van Averbeke, A.W. Ivling, H.S. James, C.A. Jones, Frederick C. Moorey, I.S. Price, Frank Scriven and Alan R. Hill.

A modest enough office staff to manage the Morel fleet of six modern ships, for by 1929 all the steamships they owned with the exception of the *Rhymney* of 1912 had been built after 1923. In the boom year of 1926 they cannot but have made very considerable profits. Having paid for these ships the Firm still had huge capital reserves and a scheme was devised to seek Chancery permission to reduce their capital. The petition was heard by Mr. Justice Romer in February of 1929. It was reported in the *Western Mail* that:

'This was a petition to confirm the reduction of the capital of the company which involved a return to the shareholders of £80 per share in respect of 5,000 shares of £100 each.

The return of the capital was proposed because there were assets amounting to £400,000 in excess of the wants of the company.

Evidence in support of the petition was contained in an affidavit by Mr. Tom Morel, a director of the Company, who established the fact that there were very large accumulated profits in reserve. The company had investments in British and Colonial stocks amounting to £262,000 investments in Public Companies and Railways amounting to £103,000, and they had in addition investments in steamships which in the last balance sheet amounted to £86,000. These were so conservatively valued, however, that the true value was £400,000.

Further they had debts owing amounting to £32,000 and a cash balance of over £13,000.

It was proposed to raise the £400,000 by selling investments to the value of £365,000, obtaining payment of £30,000 of the debts and to withdraw £5,000 in cash. Mr. Justice Romer confirmed the reduction.'

This large amount was paid out to the shareholders and in the same transaction the capital of the Company was increased again to the original £500,000 by the creation of new shares issued to the shareholders at par.

At the Fortieth Annual General Meeting in 1928 Tom Morel's son, Ted 'being a member of the Firm of Morel Brothers and Company' was appointed a director of Morel Limited.

Ted, now aged 28, worked in the London office. He had been educated at the Leys School, Cambridge which had been founded from the first as a Methodist public school to make it unnecessary for boys from Methodist homes, whose parents wanted a public school education for their sons as a preparation for entrance to Cambridge, to attend Anglican schools and so become alienated from the Church of their fathers. This pattern was followed by all the third generation Morel boys with greater or less success in their university examinations. For the girls, however, preference was given to the more fashionable Roedean or Heathfield, followed by a finishing school in Paris and their Presentation at Court — a somewhat untypical Methodist progression.

Ted Morel was a brilliant games player both at school and the University, gaining his Blue for rugby, playing for the Barbarians and representing Wales at hockey on a number of occasions. He married Phyllis Holloway of a distinguished London Methodist family and he became the Firm's family representative on the Baltic Exchange in London, continuing to play games keenly but not to the detriment of his business career. He was much liked and respected as a wealthy young man with great expectations who was still prepared to do a good day's work in the family firm.

Toward the end of 1929 steps were taken to capitalize a further £400,000, 'part of the undivided profits of the Company standing to the credit of the Investments Appreciation Account.' This amount, as in the case of the

SS Rhymney, built in 1912 for Lunsford Steamship Company. Acquired by Morel Limited in 1922.

SS Pontypridd, the second, built in 1924 by the Northumberland Steamship Company Newcastle, laid up at Fowey in September, 1924.

previous distribution, was divided between the five shareholders, the five children of Thomas Morel now in their fifties, and was to be 'treated for all purposes as an increase of the nominal amount of capital of the Company held by each shareholder and not as income.'

It would seem that, at this time, the activities of Morel Limited as an investment company were as considerable as its involvement in shipping.

In 1930 the dividend was passed and in 1931 for the first time in the minute book of the Company comments on the depressed state of shipping were recorded.

> 'The Directors reported that the business of the Companies under their management had been carried on with reasonable success in face of extremely adverse market conditions and in the case of the Treherbert Steamship Company Limited they had agreed to forgo all remuneration in respect of Management Commission and Brokerage on the earnings of that Company for the year ending 31st March, 1931.'

In 1932

> 'The Directors reported that conditions in the Shipping Industry during the past year continued very depressed.'

When all seamen's wages were reduced by 10% in 1932, the office staff of Morel Limited suffered a similar reduction. Ronald Hunt, who had joined the Firm in 1931 as junior clerk at 10/- per week, had his wages cut to 9/- a week in 1932. In 1933, on becoming 18, he had to pay his share of his National Insurance Contribution which reduced his wage to 8/- a week.

Consequently he left the Firm and obtained a similar position at 15/- a week, rising quickly to £1, with the Reardon Smith Company with whom he remained for the next 40 years.

In 1933, the Articles of Association were altered to allow the directors of Morel Limited to consist of 'not less than one nor more than five members or shareholders.' This was passed to enable the elder son of Ralph Morel — Bill — to become a director. Bill had been brought up at St. Andrews and had spent a very great deal of his youth with horses — hunting, point-to-point races and steeple-chasing — and when up at Cambridge was to be seen more often at Newmarket than was conducive to the getting of a degree. He was the favourite nephew of his uncle, Major Clem Morel, who alternately indulged him by giving him a free hand at Tullamine Castle, County Tipperary, whilst he, Clem, was sailing either his fine weather or his bad weather yacht on the Broads, or blamed him because he was making what Clem considered were the wrong friends. However, his uncle expected him to dance attendance on him both in Ireland and Norfolk and his consequent absences from Cardiff did little to endear him to the other directors of the Firm. The Clem Morels were childless and they had made the three Ralph Morel children their heirs, but the

Steel from the Dowlais Works at East Moors, used in ship repairing by the Morel firm in their Bute Graving Docks. Circa 1927. Tom Morel and Ralph Morel, the two senior directors, stand towards the centre of the photograph.

relationship with Bill was a difficult one, eventually breaking down, and he was cut out of his uncle's will.

In 1933 Tom Morel was pricked as High Sheriff of Glamorgan. It was unusual at that time for a member of other than the Anglican Communion to hold this high office. The duties were largely nominal except for entertaining and supporting the Judges as they presided over the Assizes. The usual practice is for the firm of which a High Sheriff is a member to carry a considerable amount of the expenses of the office, and this Morel Limited did. Tom Morel chose as his Chaplain the Rev. Thomas Naylor, the Chairman of the Cardiff and Swansea District of the Methodist Church; it would never have occurred to him to have sought the support of other than a Methodist minister.

Tom's wife, Edith, had died in 1923 and in 1926 he had married Constance Boyd — the occasion for the presentation of the salver. This did not in any way change his comparatively simple pattern of living. Sundays he devoted to the church, and most early evenings on his return from the office, he took a walk along the cliffs in Penarth with his docksmen friends, Willie Hinde and Willie Leon, followed by family bridge after dinner for 'love' rather than money. For exercise, some mild golf at Southerndown on the Glamorgan coast.

He was not one, however, to enjoy paying more tax than was legally necessary and the potential tax liability of the Firm, still bulging with money, was a real concern to him.

In the early 1930s, Morel Limited considered the possibility of effecting a legal tax avoidance arrangement for their company by transferring their assets to Canada. Under the existing Canadian law a U.K. resident could transfer sterling assets to a specially incorporated personal private holding company incorporated in the Province of Prince Edward Island in exchange for a small number of shares and an issue of non interest bearing redeemable debentures. These debentures were paid into a Settlement under Prince Edward Island law with the Royal Trust Company of Canada as trustee. From time to time a proportion of the debentures was redeemed equal in value to the accumulation of income in the private personal company, and the proceeds, being capital, were remitted to the client in the United Kingdom without tax liability.

Tom and John Morel and their wives went to Canada, were received and dined by the Governor General as prominent British business men, and set up the scheme.

The five principal shareholders duly formed personal private holding companies and the assets of the Company were transferred to Canada. However, within a very short time the United Kingdom Finance Act of 1936 rendered this scheme ineffectual and the assets were brought back to Britain. Morel Limited did not explore further the possibility of tax havens. Canada had been considered a secure and friendly land where it was possible to lodge the Firm's assets; the Cayman Islands and other such havens did not appeal to the cautious Morels and they made no other attempt on these lines to solve the problem of their surplus money.

In 1934, at the annual general meeting, the directors continued to report that 'conditions in the shipping industry during the past year continued very depressed'.

Tom Morel died in June of the following year at the age of 61.

In 1896, when he had become a Director of Morel Limited, there had been 96 companies in Cardiff, owning between them 365 vessels, from small sailing ships of 55 tons to steamers of 2,700 tons. In 1919, the number of companies had fallen to 56. In the boom year of 1920 there were 115 companies, but by 1931 the number of local companies had again fallen — to 77, with a total of 313 vessels, and a still further shrinkage occurred in subsequent years.[1] In the first period he had seen, at least, 40 companies go, and in the second period, at least, 38 companies come and go, from the office at 2 Stuart Street, which was getting shabbier and more run down with every passing year, but which remained very much in business during this period.

His sister, Gladys, had made a full life for herself in her widowhood. She took a leading part in Penarth in the development of Child Welfare services, which this town pioneered outside London, creating with volunteers a service for which later the local authority took responsibility.

With her brother Tom, she was deeply involved in the children's home — the J.A. Gibbs Home — which she had created out of the old Penarth Hotel, firstly for war orphans and then for all children in need of residential care. As a Nautical School, it provided training, as the Duke of York — later George VI, said at the opening, 'for the essential calling of the Sea'.

The boys of the Home paraded with a band and in naval uniform to Trinity Church on Sunday mornings and filled the front pews. One of the boys, later when a deck officer on one of the Morel ships, revisited the Church and remembered how Mr. Tom Morel, the Chairman of the committee of the Home had worshipped Sunday by Sunday, occupying the back pew. He wondered how a man who could run his company so firmly and drive such a hard bargain with his crews, housed in the cramped fo'c'sles of the 20th century tramp steamers, could reconcile these two aspects of his life.

But Tom was a man of his generation and the inconsistencies of his life — if inconsistencies there were — were those of his class and background. He managed to keep his ships in service during the depression and to provide work for the office staff and the crews of the Morel steamers when other companies had gone into liquidation and increased the number of those on the dole. The Protestant ethic had its weaknesses but had its strengths as well.

At his death, Tom Morel left an estate with net personality of £466,273 on which estate duty of £150,986 was paid. He nominated his son Ted to succeed him as a member of Morel Brothers and Company and as the Director of Morel Limited — which steps had, in fact, been taken during his lifetime in 1928.

CHAPTER TEN

John Morel's Chairmanship 1935-1948

The First Period

John Morel was elected in 1935 as the Chairman of Morel Limited. In strict order of seniority the Chair should have passed to Ralph Morel but he was sitting increasingly loosely to his responsibilities to the Firm. The South Wales press showed him 'Leading in his winner at the Glamorgan Steeplechase', 'Toasting the success of Buckbasket which won the hurdle-race at 100 to 6 at Colwell Park Races', 'Chatting in the Paddock at Cowbridge', 'In the Director's Box at Chepstow Race Course', 'Presiding at the Vale of Glamorgan Agricultural Society Meeting', 'Aboard his yacht *The Breeze* in Porlock Harbour'.

His qualifications as a naval architect and engineer were less and less employed in the service of the Firm. On his death the *Western Mail* wrote of him 'he will be remembered for his long associations with horse racing and the hunting field' which rather unfairly ignored his earlier contributions to the Firm.

He was generous and warm-hearted but, at times, an embarrassment to his family. For example in 1925, when Tom was taking his son, Ted, and his fiancée to dinner with Mrs. Robert Gibbs at The Croft, Dinas Powis, they were met by a car lurching from side to side along the narrow hedge-lined road. The driver was clearly very drunk and Tom's chauffeur, Goddard, had great difficulty in avoiding the oncoming car. Tom's embarrassment was considerable in having to admit to his future daughter-in-law that the driver was his younger brother, Ralph, from St. Andrew's House.

Morel Brothers and Co at this date consisted of directors: John G. Morel, Ralph E. Morel, Ted Morel and Bill Morel. The staff were: C.J. Hill in the London office, Secretary, William H. Johnson, Manager, Harold S. Rees, Engineer, Tom Fox, with H.J. Price, Cyril H. Jones, Terrence Thomas and Vivian Whitson.

John Morel was the obvious choice for the new chairman, being the able brother who had sat close to the business and, in the main, Ralph conceded this. John was driven to the Docks five days a week by his chauffeur, Vokings, previously his father's coachman, from his country house, Henstaff Court in the Vale of Glamorgan. Apart from shipping, his interests were his home, which he furnished with fine antiques, and his garden with its long herbaceous borders and croquet lawn, on which attempting to make the ball jump was prohibited in the interests of the turf. In the home farm attached to the house he had a pedigree herd of Red Poll cattle. He ran his farm at a tax-deductible loss until the time when the tax inspector would not accept the Red Polls as a legitimate deductible expense.

With his Cory brothers-in-law he rented the Dunraven Castle Shoot. He hunted with the Glamorgan Hounds until his middle years. He was a private person with few friends.

John Morel was a hard business man, but his hardness was not absolute. Alan Hill recalls that at one time he was trying to fix the m.v. *Catrine* from West Australia to Beigh Castle on the Shannon River in Ireland. Alan Walton, a grain speculator who made his money by undercutting the big grain houses, had already bought and sold a cargo of bulk wheat from Western Australia and needed a ship to lift the cargo from there to Beigh Castle. The current market price was 92/6d per ton and the *Catrine* was the only vessel available that could lift the cargo from Australia to Ireland. Knowing the position, Morels asked 100/ – per ton. Alan Walton was forced to accept this and the vessel was fixed at that price. He told Morels that because of the rate he had speculated for the cargo, he would not make any profit on the deal and this information reached John Morel. 'I don't want anyone to work for me for nothing; I will give him 1¼ % commission'. Alan Walton was very thankful and as a result fixed several more similar cargoes with the Morel Firm, which John Morel had not particularly intended.

The transaction illustrates nicely the relationship between the ship's brokers and managers, Morel Brothers and Company, and the owners of the cargo, who in this case had actually sold it before ensuring that they had a bottom in which to carry it to the port of discharge.

Tom knew the character of his brother John and the strain that his style of chairmanship of the Firm must bring for his son. He left a letter for Ted 'not to be opened until after my death' which stated that John would be a very difficult person with whom to work and that if Ted so wished he must feel quite free to resign from Morel Limited. Ted was indeed to find the relationship very difficult for the next twenty-one years, but he did not resign and remained as co-Director with his uncle until the end of the Firm.

Ted Morel, with Charles Hill, was in charge of the London office in which more and more of the actual day to day decisions of the Firm were taken. Ted had given up his rugby and hockey and developed his interest in golf and bridge, at both of which games he was almost as successful as he had been in the former field games. He had two daughters and this, added to the fact that John Morel's only child was also a girl, Mary, had far reaching effects on the future of the Firm; the succession was not assured in the male line, and the drive to continue the business was running down.

Bill Morel was a Director, but his involvement in the everyday workings of the Firm was very slight. If he was not being at the beck and call of his Uncle

Clem, he was riding his father's horses as an amateur jockey, or on the yacht *The Breeze*, sailing in the Bristol Channel from Barry to Porlock. He even went so far as to commission a boat from the well-known builder, Uffa Fox, *The Fresh Breeze*, but this was not completed until after his death in 1951 and he was never able to take delivery of her. In 1947 he had sold all his shareholding in Morel Limited, being the one-third of his father's share which had been passed to him a number of years previously, for £30,000 to the wholly owned subsidiary of Morel Limited, the Pontypridd Steam Ship Company, and thus severed all connection with the Firm. As the shares were in a private company the market for them was restricted and he received less than one tenth of their potential value. He moved to Porlock in Somerset and became the landlord of the Porlock Arms.

His younger brother, Clement, had been working in the Firm at the times of his brother's absences; a less satisfactory arrangement can hardly be imagined. Clement, however, showed very little interest in becoming deeply involved in shipping, so the Ralph Morel's claim to a place in Morel Brothers & Company, and to a directorship on the Morel Board, went by default.

At the Forty-seventh Annual Meeting in 1935 'the Directors reported that conditions in the Shipping Industry during the past year showed a slight improvement'. It was in this year that the Company embarked on a programme of expansion and decided to order seven new vessels from William Doxford & Sons of Sunderland. The first was the motor vessel the *Jersey*, of 9,175 tons, which was built at a cost of £100,000 and came into service in 1937. The Directors reported in 1937 that 'conditions in the Shipping Industry during the past year continued to show improvement.' It was the period of the Spanish Civil War.

On March 11th, 1938, at a directors' meeting attended by John and Ted Morel; 'in consequence of the report of the unsatisfactory trading results of the Pontypridd and Treherbert Steamship Companies, the Directors agreed to waive the Management Commission and Brokerage due to the Company from 19th February 1937 and the 7th January 1937 respectively, and that in the circumstances all Management Commission and Brokerage due from these Companies in the future be waived until further notice'.

The Fifty-second Annual General Meeting in 1940 was attended by Mary Lewin, John Morel's only daughter, and by a representative of the Estate of the late Clem Morel. Clem, Thomas Morel's third son, died aboard his yacht *Black Joke* lying in Brixham Harbour in his sixty-second year. He had given up his houses in Ireland and Norfolk and was living at Steadlings, Alveston, Gloucestershire. He left £192,846, with estate duty of £51,037, a considerably smaller estate than either of his brothers, but, not being a member of Morel Brothers & Company, or a Director of Morel Limited, he had not shared in the

SS Nolisement, the third, built in 1928 by the Northumberland Steamship Company.

MV Forest, built 1937 by W. Doxford and Sons, Sunderland. Photograph taken in 1948/49.

profits of the Management Company, nor in the Directors' Fees of Morel Limited. He enjoyed an extremely high standard of living. Everything had to be of the very best, guns by Holland & Holland, and suits by Huntsman's. To his Ralph Morel nephews and nieces he had seemed in his prime to be the 'super gentleman'.

He died childless, leaving his estate half to his nephew Clement, and half to his niece Posy and her son Ifor. He left his race-horses to his niece. The *Western Mail*, after leading in bold type with the total of his estate, added that he was 'a partner in the firm of Cardiff Shipowners' which was not, in fact, the case.

The appearance of other than the immediate family at the annual general meeting in 1940 was a shock to the directors as the realization dawned on John and Ted that they were minority shareholders in a private company and that, if there were to be a confrontation, they could be outvoted by the other shareholders and could lose their offices and their control of the Company.

There was, however, no imminent likelihood of this; the Second World War was no time for family manoeuvrings or a showdown, and there was no move in this direction.

In September 1939 at the onset of the Second World War all ocean-going British ships were requisitioned. Morel Limited continued to own ships and Morel Brothers and Company to manage them, and during the war years from 1942 onwards disclosed at the annual general meetings the result of the trading for the previous year:—

1942 — a profit of £495.17.1 subject to taxation
1943 — a profit of £13,189.6.2 subject to taxation
1944 — a profit of £7,753.17.5 subject to taxation
1945 — a profit of £14,358.8.1 subject to taxation
1946 — a profit of £15,919.9.9 — it was proposed to reserve for taxation £6,420.15.0
1947 — a profit of £14,745.2.1 — subject to taxation

These profits were those from the management activities of the Firm only, as during the war all trading profits accrued to H.M. Government.

The Firm entered the 1939-1945 war with three steamships and two new motor vessels, the M.V. *Jersey* and the M.V. *Forest*. Two of the steamships were sunk as was the *Jersey*, and the *Forest* was damaged by enemy action in 1942.

In 1940 a new Manager, Alan Roberts, had been appointed to the Cardiff office, following on the premature retirement through illness of Harold Rees. Alan Roberts was with the Guardian Line in Cardiff. Morels had been unable to trade their SS *Rhymney* profitably and they sold her to the Guardian Line. Within a year, Alan Roberts had resold her at a considerable profit to a Hong

Kong company. John Morel was incensed, but on reflection decided that if Alan Roberts was so smart then he could be smart on behalf of Morel Limited, and he invited him to join the Firm and to take over the day-to-day running of the Company.

The responsibility of the Manager in Cardiff was paralleled by that of Charles Hill as Manager in London, and he worked with Morel Limited in all for 56 years.

The amount of responsibility undertaken by the Directors and by the Managers varied; decisions of major importance were taken by the Directors. The actual decision making was by consensus; when each respected the other's ability, which in the main applied, this worked reasonably well. John and Ted complained that Alan Roberts, on Charles Hill's retirement, assumed too much. To Alan Roberts, John and Ted did nothing and let him do the worrying. This he did not mind, but what really irked him was when Ralph Morel treated him, as he did on occasion, with contempt.

In 1941, the Ministry of War Transport placed the management of four vessels in the hands of the Company following its normal war-time practice: the MV *Empire of Sidney* and the SS *Ocean Merchant*, the SS *Fort McMurray* and the SS *Fort Fairford*.

Morel Limited actually took possession in 1943 of the *Jersey Hart* ordered in 1935 and built for them during the War. Ted Morel was fearful of the possible glut in shipping which might occur after the war, especially if the American Liberty ships came onto the market. In Alan Robert's terms, 'he lost his nerve' and although John Morel and Alan Roberts did their best to dissuade him, he insisted on her sale in the following year.

It was at their annual general meetings that the family tensions became overt. On one occasion Ralph Morel seated himself in the Chair in the first-floor Board Room at 2 Stuart Street, stating that it was his right as the eldest Director. John Morel rushed down the stairs shouting that he had been insulted; it was all his sister and daughter could do to calm him down and persuade him to return and take the Chair which had meanwhile been grudgingly vacated by his brother. On this occasion there were nine members of the family present and not enough office chairs for them to sit down, so the Firm had borrowed four red and black painted chairs from an amateur drama group. The accommodation at 2 Stuart Street was becoming increasingly run down but the Directors were content that this should be so and that they should make no attempt to vie with the refurbished offices around. The symbol of the Firm's status was the date of founding — 1856, as it continued to proclaim somewhat erroneously on its cheques — rather than in the buildings from which the Firm operated.

The increased number of shareholders present at the annual general meetings reflected in different ways the irreconcilable interests of the members of the Firm and the lack of a common policy amongst the Directors. Ted Morel advised Alan Hill, son of Charles Hill, who had been in the London office since 1926 and had left the firm in 1939, to return on his demobilisation in 1945 to his pre call-up job with the Ministry of Transport, rather than return to Morel Limited. He was concerned that the Firm might well break up and there would be nothing for Alan Hill in Morel Limited within a short time.

The Directors began the practice of issuing proxy forms to be filled in by members who could not attend annual general meetings in case interests polarised and groups formed and it was required that votes rather than hands be counted to confirm the directors in office.

In 1945 Morel Limited had a great deal of money. The Firm had also the right to receive insurance monies for the SS *Pontypridd* and the SS *Jersey*, both of which had been sunk in the war. This compensation could only be paid out against the ordering of new ships and this the Directors were loath to do at this juncture.

At the end of hostilities a decision was taken to close the Cardiff office completely. More and more was done from Holland House and Alan Roberts moved to London in 1945 to manage the London office on Charles Hill's retirement.

No. 2 Stuart Street was let to a number of small tenants, amongst which were the Atlas Preservation Co. Ltd. and the National Egg Board, and quickly became more and more neglected. All the subsequent annual general meetings were held in Holland House, 32 Bury Street, E.C.3, a pleasant and well situated London office, but characterless and lacking the immediate contact with the sea at Cardiff which Stuart Street afforded.

This contact with the sea at Cardiff for the Morel ships was by now almost non-existent. After its brief resurgence as a comparatively safe port during the war, the trade from and into Cardiff Docks had slumped to a fraction of its former volume. Built primarily for the export of coal, Cardiff Docks were not, without modification, suitable for the export in bulk of any other commodity and it had never been geared to a great import trade. It was a rare occasion indeed when in 1948 one of the Morel ships, the *Nolisment*, steamed up the Bristol Channel and berthed in Cardiff Docks.

From 1945 onwards John Morel had no office in Cardiff from which to work and although he still visited the Docks regularly and could continue to call himself a shipowner, it was only when he visited London and walked in to Holland House that he could really feel himself to be one. His son-in-law, Colonel Ivor Lewin, had left the Army where he had had a congenial life, and, for family reasons, had entered the London office and become a Director of the Firm, but the complications of ship management eluded him and he found it difficult, without a lifetime in shipping behind him, to master the abbreviations by which shipping men communicated with each other.

At a Directors' meeting held on December 10th 1947, the proposition was made and carried:

> 'That the Company [Morel Brothers & Co.] waives its claim to the 3% Management Commission due from the Nolisment Steamship Company Ltd. for the period from 1st April 1947 to 3rd December 1947, to the extent of £5,000; also that the offer of the Pontypridd Steamship Co. Ltd. to pay to the Company the sum of £5,000 as a special additional remuneration in recognition of the Company's successful handling of the War Damage Claim per MV Catrine be, and is hereby, gratefully accepted'.

Directors' meetings were recorded in the latter part of 1948 at which lawyers were present and plans revealed for reconstruction of the Company by means of a Members Voluntary Liquidation and the sale of the Company's undertaking and assets to a new Company to be formed for this purpose. Service agreements for John Morel, Ted Morel and Alan Roberts with the new Company were agreed.

An extraordinary general meeting on 12th October, 1948 confirmed the arrangement. The new Company, also called Morel Limited, had the same shareholders as had the former Company. In addition to being a tidying-up operation, the reconstruction was undertaken as a means of making a capital distribution to shareholders. The amount of money surplus to the requirements of the new Company was paid out to the old shareholders in a first distribution of £10 per share and a second distribution in the next year of £12 per share requiring a total of £513,326.

New 5/ – shares credited as fully paid to a total of 1,904,000 were distributed to the former old Morel Limited shareholders pro rata to their shareholdings.

The minute book ends with minutes of the meetings chaired by the liquidator of the Company in October 1948 and December 1949. By this time, the greater part of the shareholdings had been passed by the children of Thomas Morel to their children and were in the hands of cousins, only one of whom, Ted, was a Director of the Firm, and a member of the Management Company.

There could now be little sense of identity or even common interest to ensure the future of the new Company.

CHAPTER ELEVEN

The New Company 1948-1956

The Memorandum and Articles of Association of the new Morel Limited preserved its character as a private company: 'The Directors may in their absolute discretion and without assigning any reason therefore decline to register any transfer of shares to any person'.

The operations of the Company were confined to the shipping industry in its broadest terms with an extension to aircraft if this seemed to be desirable. The founding directors were John Morel, Ted Morel, Ivor Lewin and Alan Roberts, Manager, and later Alan Hill, Chartering Manager, the first three being Permanent Directors. The directors' fees were fixed at £150 per annum with an additional £350 per annum for the chairman, and it was laid down that any director who performed services which were outside the scope of the ordinary duties of a director might be paid extra remuneration at the discretion of the Board.

The Morel family were uneasy at having other than family members on the Board and it was made clear to Alan Roberts and Alan Hill that except for the additional remuneration it would make 'no difference to their position'. When the real discussion of the future of the Company took place immediately after the holding of the annual general meetings, they were expected to leave; it was, however, on their knowledge and skills that the Firm depended.

Alan Roberts described the organisation of the London office during this period:

> 'The day to day management of the Firm rested with Ted Morel, and I was the active director in daily attendance at the office, 32 Bury Street in the City. Alan Hill was the chartering director and was responsible for 'marking the market' every day. Ted and I went on the Baltic Exchange soon after noon when Alan Hill reported the state of the market. I did all the voyage estimating working out the profit per day that would result from taking any particular freight that was offered and then Alan Hill would begin negotiations with the prospective charterers. This required a knowledge of cargoes, of ports and of the weather to be expected in the various seas. Alan Hill wrote a market report every day, a copy of which was sent daily to Mr. John Morel at his home. He telephoned me at about 9.30 a.m. to discuss matters generally before Ted Morel and Ivor Lewin arrived.
>
> I carried out the negotiations when ships were sold and also agreed with the Superintendent Engineer, Elias Pearson, the specifications for the three new 'Jersey' ships.
>
> In addition there were other matters — insurances, communications with the ships' captains, recruitment of officers and crews and the decision whether to trade on a voyage or on a time charter which at this time largely fell to me.
>
> Whilst John and Ted Morel were the registered Ships Husbands with the Register of Shipping, all the directors of the Firm were members of the Baltic Exchange.'

John and Ted Morel took the major decisions in policy matters and committed themselves as much or as little as they chose in the day to day management of the Firm. With the shipbroking in competent hands and a small modern fleet, the Firm was able to take advantage of the shipping boom brought about by the Korean War in the early 1950s.

Nevertheless the family Directors, although the management problems of the Firm did not trouble them unduly, had two major concerns; the ultimate control of the Company and the huge amount of capital tied up in it.

The first united John and Ted Morel in a way they were not often united. They were uneasily aware that they would not be ultimately in control of the Company if there were to be a conflict and shareholdings were to be counted. When they mustered all the votes from their side of the family, they would have no more than two-fifths of the total votes. Gladys Gibbs, as her brothers, had passed her share to the next generation so John Morel Gibbs controlled one fifth. However, the children of Ralph Morel, Posy and Clement, had their Uncle Clem's one fifth share and two-thirds of their father's fifth share — their brother Bill's one-third of that having been sold back to a subsidiary of the Company in 1947 — so that if they joined together with John Morel Gibbs, they would be able to out-vote John and Ted Morel at a general meeting. For this to come to pass a great deal of planning and plotting would have been necessary and it was in fact most unlikely that they would take any such action. Posy and Clem were occupied in county pursuits and John Morel Gibbs was teaching in University College, Cardiff.

However, the fear remained and in May 1949 Ted wrote to John Morel Gibbs informing him that at a meeting of the Board of Directors, it was unanimously decided to invite him to join the Board of Morel Limited. He went on:

> 'Our business is of necessity conducted on a day to day basis and it is therefore not the practice to hold regular Board meetings.
>
> If circumstances should, however, demand an immediate meeting of the Board and time not permit of your attendance, a copy of the Minutes would be immediately sent to you.'

John Morel Gibbs accepted the invitation and he was made a Director on 28th July, 1949. In a sense the Morels were eating their words as a Gibbs was now a director, but it was made clear to him in the letter of invitation that his involvement in the day-to-day running of the Firm was to be nominal. He was never called to a Directors' meeting nor did he receive any director's fees. In effect, the Firm forgot about the arrangement. However, John and Ted Morel presumably slept more easily at night thereafter,

Susan Gladys Gibbs died in 1952. She remained a very good Methodist all her life becoming a Circuit Steward, an unusual honour and responsibility for a woman. She had avoided the temptation of keeping her only son at home with her as Fanny, Mrs. Robert Gibbs, had done with her only son, Alan, to his considerable disadvantage, and also rejected the advice to 'pack him off to the Shires with a couple of good hunters' proffered by the more sporting of her brothers. Her nieces called her 'Aunt Glad, the Good' in contrast to Clem's wife 'Aunt Glad, the Bad', but her goodness was never oppressive.

Along with her brother Tom, she invested some of the money she received from Morel Limited in property in Cardiff, notably Merthyr House at the Docks and Dominions House in Queen Street and she also set up a charitable trust. She always maintained a lively interest in her family Firm.

The Company minute book for this period is not extant but Alan Roberts has provided the following information. The former policy of low yearly dividends with capital disbursements when legally possible was maintained by the new Company. From its incorporation onwards, a dividend of 2½% was paid in 1949 and then of 1% from 1950 until 1954, in spite of the boom in shipping from 1950 onwards. A dividend of 10% was declared in 1955. No dividend was paid in 1956, although there was a distribution of capital of £250,000 in that year to the shareholders.

The *Journal of Commerce, Shipbuilding and Engineering* of November 25th, 1943 had written on the occasion of the transfer of the motorship the *Empire Sidney*, which had been managed during the War by Morel Limited, to the Netherlands Shipping and Trading Company Limited that:

> 'Messrs. Morel were among a small group of ambitious owners who just prior to the outbreak of the war were convinced of the possibilities of the standard oil-engined tramp of about 9,000 tons deadweight.'

These motor ships referred to in the *Journal of Commerce* article formed the basis of the Morel Fleet in the 1950's. The last three were contracted for in 1951, the *Jersey Spray*, the *Jersey Dawn* and the *Jersey Mist*.

All three ships were launched in 1953 and their dimensions show that they were, for that time, big ships of 9,175 net tons, length 420 ft., breadth 57′9″ and depth 28′6″. Insurance monies received under Government Tonnage Replacement Act of 1940 following on the sinking of the four Morel ships in the Second World War, was put towards the payment for these new ships. At the launch of the *Jersey Mist* Ted Morel said he 'was proud to think that a ship as big as this could in these days be built for a private firm'. The *Jersey Mist* cost over £500,000. The specification indicated that she was intended for General Cargo — Worldwide, that all accommodation was to be amidships and that she would be worked by a Lascar crew. The last three ships ordered had all been so specified. Alan Roberts said that the decision on this last point was taken because a Lascar crew maintained the ship to a very high standard and remained on board in British ports. The cost of such a crew was not very different from that of a British crew as considerably more Lascar sailors were

MV Jersey Dawn built for Morel Limited in 1953 by W. Pickersgill and Sons of Sunderland.

The launching of The Jersey Dawn in 1953, from the yard of W. Pickersgill and Sons Sunderland.

employed, but it is an indication of the difficulties involved in manning ships with British crews that the decision as to the type of crew that would be carried was pre-empted in this way. The crew, who had a Bhandary, an overseer, was recruited in Calcutta, flown out to the ship at a convenient port and then taken back to India by air at the end of the term of service.

The office staff at this time consisted of no more than four men: Alan Roberts and Alan Hill, Harold Halsey, the accountant, and Elias Pearson, the superintendent engineer with clerical assistants. Morel Limited always stretched and sometimes overstretched, their office staff.

With these three very modern motor vessels in service the future of the Firm looked assured, but the question of the succession and of the future management loomed ahead. In 1955 John Morel was 72 years old and Ted 55. John, now that 2 Stuart Street had been abandoned, could be involved only in the Firm's day to day decisions by telephone or when staying up in London at the Mayfair Hotel, by dropping in on the City Office. Ted had developed rather late in life a keen interest in horse racing, and was tired of working in a Firm which often brought little pleasure. He was increasingly unwilling to carry the responsibility for the Firm; in addition to his own, there was so much of his cousins' capital tied up in it and they were getting increasingly anxious. What would happen to their estates if they were to die with their major holding in a private company which could not be realised but which would inevitably be assessed for death duty purposes at a considerable figure?

The parcels of shares had so far been passed successfully from hand to hand down through the generations, but now, with the enormous potential tax liability no member wished to be left holding the parcel, as it were, when the music stopped. At any moment, any of the beneficiaries — even quite a young one — might die and the contents of the parcel be spilled with not only heavy death duties to face but few means of meeting them except at the expense of other parcel holders.

The possibility of becoming a public company was considered; if this were done the shares would have been negotiable at any time although the market would have been somewhat restricted. John Morel, however, was not prepared to account to a public annual general meeting; 'I'm not going public and have every Tom, Dick and Harry telling me what to do'.

There was one young male Morel who might yet come into the Firm and provide the succession; Michael, Clement Morel's elder son. By invitation he moved up to London and started to work in the office. Ted Morel never felt that this could really be the solution to the future of the Firm and never gave Michael the encouragement he needed to become identified with the Company and interested in shipping. For Ted, the issue was not whether or no there was a young Morel working in the office; it was that he himself had to carry the responsibility for the huge capital investment that the four very valuable ships represented. Michael was eager to get away from London and home for weekends and in less than a year he had moved back to South Wales and become articled in a solicitors' firm in Cardiff.

There would have been one other solution open to John and Ted Morel if they had wished Morels to remain a family firm and that was to turn to the Gibbs relations.

There had been no question of Gladys Morel's son, John Morel Gibbs, going into Morel Limited as a career even if he had shown an interest in so doing — 'Impossible! he was a Gibbs', as Ted Morel said.

In the 1950s there were two grandsons of John Angel Gibbs engaged in shipping in their own Firm, Gibbs and Company; Nigel and Vivian Gibbs and they were making a success of their Company. They had also however, the same fatal drawback — their name. Although John Morel's middle name was Gibbs and his mother had been a Gibbs and his sister had married one, he could not allow the possibility of a Gibbs becoming the Chairman of Morel Limited. The matter was discussed amongst the Morels but no approach was ever made.

Ted Morel was increasingly sure that the only solution was for the Firm to come to an end. John Morel had no other solution; and one shareholder was taking advice from the House of Rothschild on the position of a major shareholder tied into a private company.

The issue became how and when this was to happen. Matters were allowed to drift until John Morel met a South Wales friend, H.H. Merrett, the financier, in the Mayfair Hotel and asked him casually whether he would be interested in buying the four Morel ships. H.H. Merrett showed an interest in the proposition and Alan Roberts went to Cwrt-y-ala House outside Cardiff, H.H. Merrett's home, with the Firm's balance sheets to discuss the matter further. A figure for purchasing the ships was suggested which the Directors did not consider adequate and they made a counter proposal which H.H. Merrett was to put to his Board, the Powell Duffryn Company.

The Morel family was alerted and all gathered one afternoon at Henstaff Court to hear the result of the deliberations and to vote on the issue if the response were positive.

The family whiled away the afternoon playing some desultory hands of bridge and then the news was 'phoned through that the Powell Duffryn Board was not prepared to go forward on the Morels' terms. The family dispersed.

Matters dragged on; a slump seemed to be setting in and there was no movement until the Suez crisis occurred. As ever, in a situation of increased international tension the threat to the Canal caused interest in ships and shipping to flare up, and the ships were sold. The timing of the operation was entirely fortuitous, brought about by events quite beyond Morel family control.

The *Evening Post* of Jersey on 23rd March, 1956 recorded the event as of interest to the Island;

> 'Three Jersey ships will no longer carry the Island's good name around the world. Known as *'Jersey Spray'*, *'Jersey Dawn'* and *'Jersey Mist'* they were named after the Island because the owners' family came from there. But the owners, Morel Ltd. of London, one of the few private shipping firms left in Britain are selling them. Their new owners will give them new names. The *'Jersey Dawn'*, 5,342 tons, has been sold to the Scindia Steam Navigation Co. Ltd. of Bombay for £850,000 and negotiations have been nearly completed for the sale of the *'Jersey Mist'*, 5,484 tons, and the *'Jersey Spray'*, 5,488 tons, to a Canadian firm for about £840,000 each. The prices are higher than those for a new ship — the three were built in 1953/54 — but the buyers would have to wait from two to three years to have one built. Morel Ltd. now have only one ship left, the *'Catrine'*.'

The sale of the *Catrine* is documented in *Lloyd's List and Shipping Gazette* for 4th July, 1956.

> 'Very few inter-British sales have been concluded during the quarter. The last unit of the fleet of Morel Ltd. the *'Catrine'* (9,462 tons and built 1940) was sold to Hong Kong buyers at £465,000 including charter — a sad reminder of the prevailing tendency of British tramp owners to sell rather than buy and an ominous commentary on the dangerous effect of penal taxation on a highly competitive industry.'

The Company began to be wound up in 1956. Ted Morel and A.W. Ponder were appointed liquidators, although Alan Roberts arranged all the matters for the liquidation. After reserving what was required for tax, distributions of the capital were made over the ensuing years to the shareholders. The last distribution being made on 29th January, 1960.

The five children of Thomas Morel and their children and grandchildren were the principal beneficiaries, but there remained a number of the original shareholders who had taken up one or two shares in the Morel ships in the 19th century and who had resisted all overtures made from time to time by the Directors to buy them back, although the sole remaining French shareholder, Madame Le Ronde, sold her shares to Ted Morel in 1955.

Of the members of the Firm, John Morel and Ted Morel retired, the former keenly aware that he had lost his status and role as shipowner. Alan Roberts retired also at 61 years, several years before he felt it appropriate so to do. Alan Hill, ship charterer in his own right, moved on to Matthews, Wrightson and eventually to Gibbs and Co. to work alongside and indeed, with, the second generation directors of Gibbs and Co.

John Morel summed up the ending of Morel Limited in the following letter written to his cousin, Arthur Morel, in Jersey:

'29th March, 1956

Dear Arthur,

The family have decided to wind up Morel Limited. Naturally it is a bitter blow for me as I am the last of the generation which had so much to do with the fortunes of the Company. Unfortunately there was only one young Morel who could have carried on the Firm, but after six months in the London Office, he came out and said he had no intention of working as a shipowner.

In the last few years the Company has been more prosperous than anyone could have imagined; in fact, the profits have been really embarrassing. The three 'Jersey' ships have been absolute money spinners ably supported by the '*Catrine*' (we called this vessel after one of the old family Christian names) but the taxation law that has been passed made it impossible for a private company such as ours with only five groups of shareholders to survive. It meant that the Inland Revenue was taking practically all our profits and what the family dreaded was the impact of death duties on the very high value the Government would have insisted upon and the impossibility of selling their holding to cover the liability. . . . We have been overwhelmed by the remarks of regret both on the London Baltic and the Cardiff Exchange at the liquidation of the Company.'

John Morel died in April 1971. He would have been gratified to know that his estate was worth considerably more than those of his elder brothers, but probably not that it attracted death duties at more than eighty five per cent. It was during his Chairmanship that the move away from coal-fired to oil-fired boilers was taken; a step in line with the general trend, but which the more conservative of the Cardiff shipowners were loath to take.

It is noteworthy that the article in the *Evening Post* of Jersey referred to Morel Limited 'of London'; it was as if the Welsh connection had never been.

Stuart Street has been completely demolished and although an attempt was made in 1972 to preserve No. 2 as an example of a 19th century shipping office, architects decided that it had deteriorated too far for restoration to be possible.

CHAPTER TWELVE

After 1957: Postcript

With the end of the Morel Firm the family fell apart. By the third generation there was little but their shareholding in the Firm to hold them together and when the members were no longer called to the London office for the annual general meeting they ceased to meet even for this occasion, although a shared and deep interest in horses continued to hold two or three of the individual families together.

The houses with which they had been associated were pulled down or went out of the family. The Lindens was sold on Susanna Morel's death, becoming eventually a special school. St. Andrews House was split up into a number of living units. Penarth House, after being empty for a number of years, was demolished to make way for five houses and two residential communities, one of which for elderly people carries the name Morel Court. Roxburgh, Tom Morel's house, was demolished on his widow's death and replaced by a court of town houses. Henstaff Court, the John Morel's home, was sold on his death to a South Wales industrialist. Ted and Phyllis Morel had moved into a smaller house in the Tadworth area of Surrey with an Italian couple to look after them and the house, before the strain of their large Surrey home with nine bedrooms had become too much for them. Gladys Gibbs's house in Marine Parade was large enough to be divided on her death to make five housing units for retired Methodist ministers.

The families' standards of living declined from the outbreak of war in 1939 in company with those of others in similar positions and continued to decline steadily in subsequent years. The Morels were intelligent enough to make outrageous statements well aware of the latent humour contained in them. John Morel declared that he couldn't understand what all the talk from the 1950s onwards of a rising standard of living was all about. 'As far as I'm concerned my standard of living has been falling ever since the 1930s.' On the outbreak of war, Ted Morel decided that they must economise and then and there resolved to make his clean shirts last for two days, as he wore them to the City, and to cease taking *The Methodist Recorder*. He took neither of these steps.

But their standard of living did fall and this was particularly the case in the size of their establishments. Their houses were never stately homes nor were their establishments grand. Gladys Gibbs who lived somewhat more modestly than her brothers employed a cook, parlour maid, house maid and between-maid in the house and a chauffeur and two gardeners outside. Her brothers, apart from their stables, lived on much the same scale with the addition of an indoor man servant. Even with only one child it was assumed that a nanny would be employed and many mothers, Gladys especially, regretted that this tended to distance them from their children.

Wages were low by later standards, but the members of staff were not overworked and were glad to find a congenial place in Penarth or the Vale so near their homes, for highly populated Glamorgan was limited in the openings it could provide for women and girls. Penarth and the Vale were attractive settings compared with employment in London or big isolated country houses.

Although the terms, 'Master' and 'Mistress' were used, the relationship between the family and the staff were often extremely friendly and the children would know and visit the maids' families and play golf or go ferreting with the chauffeurs or gardeners. Whilst it was a structured relationship, it allowed for the expression of mutual respect and consideration.

Mr. Jack Hart, formerly the coachman and later the chauffeur to John and Gladys Gibbs would tell how, during the First World War on coming to work one morning somewhat later than usual, he was reprimanded by Major Gibbs: 'Have you seen the car, sir?', he said, 'We got in at 2 a.m. last night and it was not until 4 a.m. that I got to bed after drying and polishing it.' He added that Major Gibbs apologised to him. A simple anecdote which indicated an attitude of respect on both sides and, incidentally, treatment for a car very similar to that which would have been accorded to the horses and carriage earlier in the century.

Membership of the Methodist Church, which had been a uniting bond in the first generation of the family, became less significant when the members of the family began to move out into the country, where it was replaced by an adherence to Anglicanism, not infrequently, nominal in character.

The rejection of Methodism had, however, become overt by the second generation. The first two babies born to Willie and Edith Morel were baptised at Trinity Methodist Church in 1907 and 1909, but when the time came for their third child to be baptised this took place at All Saints Anglican Church in Penarth, surely at Edith's instigation. This must have caused hurt to most of the senior members of the family, but Edith could not accept her husband's denominational background. She was happy to describe her father-in-law, Philip, as 'a fine Huguenot gentleman'; she could not admit that he was a Wesleyan of Liberal persuasions. By the third generation, apart from Tom Morel's and Gladys Gibbs's family, the Methodist connection had been broken. Insofar as denominational religious observance was a significant factor in the nineteenth century, its passing cannot but have contributed to the loosening of family ties.

The ownership and management of ships had brought a fortune to each of the five branches of Thomas Morel's family. The level of taxation, however, both on income and on the transfer of capital, had inexorably eaten into these every year since 1957 when the Firm ceased to trade, went into liquidation and the capital was finally distributed to the shareholders.

The Morels have all but left South Wales. The Philip Morels had all moved away in 1919 when they were bought out of the Firm. Of Thomas Morel's descendants, Ralph's daughter Posy and her son Ifor Lewis are farming at Llantwit Major. Clement's son, Ralph, is a solicitor at St. Brides and John Morel Gibbs lives in Penarth. They are scattered families, distantly connected, who happen to bear the name Morel, with memories that become hazier with each generation, of belonging to a once prominent family that rose with the rise of Cardiff and contributed in some measure to that rise. They communicate if at all, by Christmas cards, taking only a desultory interest in the fact that one of their younger relations had gone into the Army, or into catering or into managing the race course in Cyprus.

In commercial terms the wheel turned full circle when, on the nationalization of the South Wales ports, coal ceased to be exported from Cardiff, and coal exports were concentrated at Barry and Swansea. The *South Wales Echo* carried on 24th February, 1955 a picture of the French vessel, the *Corflow*, 'discharging the first cargo of French coal at Newport Docks for the Uskmouth Power Station'.

Jean, Thomas and Philip Morel could not have imagined such a reversal of circumstances.

Their old home, Stuart Farm, in Jersey passed into the possession of Marie and Alla Goldsworthy through their mother and these two stalwart Methodists, one a missionary and the other a physiotherapist, left it, after a life tenancy to their niece, Mary le Morel, to their tenant, the French speaking farmer M. Dréan, a Breton, who works it and is bringing up his family in the old farmhouse.

Morel Farm, itself, is becoming increasingly well known. It was given by Arthur Morel, who inherited it through his mother, to the National Trust of Jersey, and the farm with its arched gateways, ciderpress, piggeries and dovecot is now one of the show places of Jersey.

Appendices

1. List of the Morel ships from 1876 to 1956

2. Valuation of Morel ships in 1885

3. A comparison between the size of the Morel Fleet and those of other contemporary Cardiff shipping firms between 1878 and 1956

4. The composition of the crews on the Morel ships in 1885 and 1905

5. The pattern of trading of the Morel ships from 1885 onwards

6. Dividends declared by Morel Limited between 1888 and 1948

7. Shares and Debentures held by Thomas Morel at his death in 1903

8. The menu, wine list and music at the complimentary Dinner to Thomas Morel in 1899

APPENDIX 1

Morel Ships 1876-1956

Period 1
1876-1888. The Move into Steam.
at 1888, 23 ships.

Period 2
1888-1903. Morel Limited.
at 1903, 25 ships.

Period 3
1903-1919.
at 1919, no ships.

Period 4
1919-1935. Tom Morel's Chairmanship.
at 1935, 4 ships.

Period 5
1935-1948. John Morel's Chairmanship.
at 1948, 3 ships.

Period 6
1948-1956. The New Company.
at 1956, no ships.

. . . .

The ships are entered with their specifications and subsequent history under the period in which they were built or acquired.

If they are owned by the Firm in a subsequent period, they are listed again by name but without details.

Period 1. 1876-1888

IS Colstrup.
Acquired 1876. Built 1874 by E.S. Swan & Co. of Newcastle.
NT 319 length 159.4 breadth 24.1 depth 14.2.
In 1887 she was sold to T.E. Brigham Newcastle. 1910 stranded at Deauville, refloated and sold for breaking up at Hartlepool.

IS Portugalette. (I)
Built in 1877 by Palmers Shipbuilding and Iron Co. Ltd. of Jarrow.
NT 371 length 180.5 breadth 26.7 depth 14.6.
1882 foundered.

IS Galdames.
Built in 1878 by Palmers of Jarrow.
NT 550 length 220 breadth 30.2 depth 15.5.
1886 wrecked.

IS Dowlais. (I)
Built in 1879 by Palmers of Jarrow.
NT 711 length 240 breadth 33.2 depth 16.0.
1904 sold to R. Craggs & Sons Middlesborough and resold to Swedish owners.
7.8.1917 torpedoed by German Submarine UC 31 in the North Sea,

IS Cyfarthfa. (I)
Built in 1880 by Palmers of Jarrow.
NT 750 length 241 breadth 33.2 depth 16.6.
1904 sold to R. Craggs & Sons Middlesborough and resold to Norgwegian owners.
24.11.1905 wrecked near Grahara on a voyage to Helsinki.

IS Beignon.
Built in 1880 by Richardson Duck of Stockton.
NT 868 length 250 breadth 25 depth 15.2.
1899 sank 3 miles from St. Nazaire following a collision whilst on a voyage from Nantes to Bilboa.

IS Forest. (I)
Built in 1880 by Palmers of Jarrow.
NT 756 length 240 breadth 33.2 depth 16.5.
Wrecked in 1887.

IS La Barrouere.
Built in 1880 by Palmers of Jarrow.
NT 773 length 241.1 breadth 33.2 depth 15.6.
25.11.1897 sunk off Lundy Island following a collision with an unknown sailing ship whilst on a voyage from Cardiff to St. Nazaire with a cargo of coal.
The captain and four crew were lost.

IS Lesraulx. (I)
Built in 1880 by W. Doxford of Sunderland.
NT 836 length 240 breadth 36 depth 16.0
1894 sold to T.G. Beatley & Son London.
26.3.1916 sunk by German Submarine U 28 in the Bay of Biscay.

IS Blaenavon. (I)
Built in 1881 by Palmers of Jarrow.
NT 842 length 240.9 breadth 33.2 depth 16.5
March 1892 posted missing on a voyage from the Clyde to Bayonne.

IS Ebbw Vale.
Built in 1881 by Palmers of Jarrow.
NT 880 length 240 breadth 33.4 depth
1891 sank off the Goodwin Sands following a collision whilst on a voyage from Bona to Dunkirk.

IS Gwentland.
Built in 1881 by J. Readhead & Co. South Shields.
NT 1012 length 250 breadth 35.2 depth 17.5
1907 sold to Norwegian owners.
1931 laid up at Oslo and sold to ship breakers.

IS Longueil.
Built by W. Pickersgill & Sons of Sunderland in 1882.
NT 1116 length 260 breadth 36.2 depth 18.0
1897 sold to German owners who in 1909 sold her to Swedish owners.
23.12.1919 wrecked at the entrance to the Manchester Ship Canal whilst on a voyage from Gothenberg.

IS Portugalette. (II)
Built in 1882 by Palmers of Jarrow.
NT 976 length 250 breadth 36.2 depth 17.3
14th May, 1901 wrecked at the entrance to Santander whilst on a voyage in ballast from St. Nazaire to Santander.

IS Rhymney.
Built in 1882 by Kish Boolds & Co. of Sunderland.
NT 930 length 240 breadth 34.1 depth 17.
3rd January, 1899 abandoned in the Bay of Biscay whilst on a voyage from Bilbao to Cardiff.

IS Merthyr.
Built in 1882 by Palmers of Jarrow.
NT 880 length 240 breadth 33.3 depth 16.8.
1906 sold to Norwegian owners.
On 27.2.1917 whilst on a voyage from Narvik to Middlesbrough after sailing from Bergen, the ship disappeared.

IS Penarth (I). (Later: IS Treherbert, (II)).
Built in 1882 by Palmers of Jarrow.
NT 1067 length 258.7 breadth 36 depth 17.3.
Some time prior to 1893 the ship had been renamed the **Treherbert. (II).**
In 1911 sold to Irish owners who later sold her to Greek owners.
On 22 April, 1941 she was bombed and sunk by German aircraft in the Gulf of Patras during the invasion of Greece.

IS Aberdare.
Built in 1882 by Palmers of Jarrow.
NT 877 length 240 breadth 33.2 depth 16.7.
In March 1899 she was sunk in collision off Barry Island whilst on a voyage from Cardiff to St. Nazaire.

IS Castanos. (I).
Built in 1882 by Oswald Mordaunt of Southampton.
NT 1113 length 25.8 breadth 36 depth 18.
In 1893 she was wrecked but subsequently salvaged and in 1894 was sold to Greek owners. In 1901 she was sold to Swedish owners and eventually in 6th June, 1917 she was torpedoed and sunk by a German submarine UC 70 in the North Sea whilst on a voyage from Grimsby to Gothenberg.

IS Collivaud. (I).
Built in 1882 by W. Doxford of Sunderland.
NT 982 length 260.6 breadth 35.3 depth 15.6.
She became stranded and later lost in 1886.

IS Gardepee.
Built in 1882 by W. Pickersgill & Sons of Sunderland.
NT 1126 length 258 breadth 36.2 depth 18.3.
She was sold in 1915 to C.A. Steward & Co. London.
On 10.10 1916 she was captured and sunk by a German submarine 70 miles NNE of North Cape whilst on a voyage from Drontheim to Archangel. All the crew were saved.

IS Tredegar.
Built in 1882 by Palmers of Jarrow.
NT 870 length 241.2 breadth 33.3 depth 16.5.
She was sold in 1908 to Spanish owners.
In March 1921 she was wrecked at Oporto Bar whilst on a voyage from Cardiff to Oporto with a cargo of coal.

IS Jersey.
Built in 1883 by Palmers of Jarrow.
NT 1056 length 260 breadth 36.2 depth 17.
She was sold in 1911 to Irish, English and eventually Welsh owners, the last being the S & R Steamships Ltd. of Llanelly. Then in 1926 they sold her to Swedish owners. On 13th December, 1942 she sank near Kiel following a collision with the German steamer Oldenberg whilst on a voyage from Vesteras to Lubeck with a cargo of iron ore.

IS Pontypridd. (I)
Built in 1883 by Blyth Shipbuilding Co. Ltd., Blyth.
NT 1092 length 260 breadth 36.1 depth 20.
She was sold in 1915 to Leadenhall Steamship Co. London, later to Wolveston Steamship Co. and eventually in 1916 to the South Metropolitan Gas Co. She was mined and sunk off Aldeburgh on 12.3.1917.

IS Allende. (later: IS Forest (II))
Built in 1883 by Palmers of Jarrow.
NT 1069 length 258.1 breadth 36.2 depth 17.3.
Following on the wrecking of the **Forest** the name of the **Allende** was changed to that of **Forest** in 1890. In 1911 she was sold to Swedish owners.
On 15th December, 1927 she was sunk off May Island following a collision whilst on a voyage from Methil to Copenhagen with a cargo of coal.

IS Treherbert. (I)
Built in 1883 by W. Pickersgill and Sons of Sunderland.
NT 1056 length 250.6 breadth 37.3 depth 17.
Wrecked in 1887.

IS Ninian Stuart.
Built in 1883 by W. Pickersgill and Sons of Sunderland.
NT 1305 length 270.2 breadth 40.3 depth 18.6.
As 'the Pride of the Fleet' she opened the Roath Dock on November 26th 1887.
In 1912 she was sold to Swedish owners.
On 11th May 1918 she was torpedoed and sunk by the German submarine UB 21 8 miles NE of Hartlepool whilst on a voyage from Hull to Blyth.

SS Collivaud. (II)
Built in 1887 by the Bute Shipbuilding, Engineering and Dry Dock Co. of Cardiff. NT 950 length 240 breadth 33.1 depth 18.
In 1912 she was sold to the New Line Steamship Company of Leith. In 1915 to S. Instone & Co. Ltd. of London and later in the same year to Balham Steamship Co. of London. In 1919 she was repurchased by the New Line Company. In 1922 she was sold to N. Fansano of Italy. In 1924 she was sold to Barzilay and Benjamin of Turkey; subsequently she had various owners under the Turkish flag and in 1934 was eventually named **Suat**. She carried this name until 1958 when she was sold to shipbreakers — after a career of 71 years.

End of Period 1.
In 1888, at the end of this period, the Morel fleet consisted of 23 ships.

Period 2. 1888-1903

In 1888, at the beginning of this period the Morel fleet consisted of:

IS Colstrup	IS Dowlais	IS Cyfarthfa	IS Beignon	IS La Barrouere
IS Lesraulx	IS Blaenavon	IS Ebbw Vale	IS Gwentland	IS Longueil
IS Portugalette	IS Rhymney	IS Merthyr	IS Penarth	IS Aberdare
IS Castanos	IS Gardépée	IS Tredegar	IS Jersey	IS Pontypridd
IS Allende		IS Ninian Stuart		SS Collivaud

Leda.
Acquired 1888 built in 1862 by Richardson Duck of Middlesborough.
NT 779 length 245 breadth 28.5 depth 17.2.
A three masted schooner formerly the **Harriet Pinkney.** Listed as a steamship by 1877 and owned by Bailey and Leetham, Hull as **Leda.** She was wrecked on 12.6.1896 near Bayonne whilst on a voyage from Nantes to Bayonne in ballast.

SS Lavernock.
Built in 1888 by Palmers of Jarrow.
NT 1482 length 275 breadth 40.3 depth 20.9.
She was sold in 1916 to Allen, Adams and Co. Ltd. of Southampton. On 17.9.1918 she was torpedoed and sunk by a German submarine 5 miles SW of Trevose Head. 25 of the crew were lost.

SS Lyndhurst.
Built in 1888 by W. Pickersgill & Sons of Sunderland.
NT 1309 length 270 breadth 40 depth 20.9.
In 1900 she was sold to the Aberdare Steamship Company of which Philip Morel was the owner and manager.
Morel Limited re-acquired her in 1907. She was sold in 1912 to Swedish owners. In January 1920 she was wrecked at Cape Finisterre whilst on a voyage form Kotka to Seville with a cargo of timber.

SS Cardiff Castle. (later: SS Blaenavon (II))
Built in 1889 by the Bute Shipbuilding, Engineering and Dry Dock Co. of Cardiff.
NT 1266 length 265.4 breadth 36.2 depth 18.4
She is not listed in the Lloyds Registry of Shipping after 1891. Following on the loss of the IS **Blaenavon** in 1892, a new **Blaenavon (II)** appears in 1894 — 'ex **Cardiff Castle**' — with the identical specification of the **Cardiff Castle** listed above. There is no indication of what happened to the **Cardiff Castle** during the years 1892 to 1894 nor why her name was changed. She was sold in 1913 to the Beechgrove Steamship Co. of Glasgow.
On 8.8.1915 she was mined off Cape Orloff whilst on a voyage from Archangel to the Clyde with a cargo of sawn goods. Later, she was beached at Slombal and became a total loss.

IS Charles W. Anderson.
Acquired in 1890. Built in 1872 by Wigham Richardson of Newcastle.
NT 1452 length 253 breadth 33.2 depth 16.1.
This three masted schooner was sold to Philip Morel in 1895 and her name changed to the **Pomaron**. In 1901 she was re-acquired by Morel Limited. She was sold in 1910 to R. White & Sons and broken up.

SS Hart.
Acquired in 1980 built in 1878 by W. Gray & Co. West Hartlepool.
NT 880 length 247 breadth 32.1 depth 18.3
She was originally built for Callender, White and Hunter of West Hartlepool.
In 1907 she was sold to J.J. King and Sons Ltd. and broken up.

SS Ferncliffe.
Acquired in 1891, built by Palmers of Jarrow in 1883 for D.H. Morgan & Co. of Newport. NT 959 length 251.3 ft. breadth 37.8 ft. depth 17.2 ft.
She was sold to Russian owners in 1893 who sold her to French owners in 1922 and later again she was sold to Turkish owners.
She was wrecked in January 1931.

SS Goldcliffe.
Acquired in 1891, built by Palmers of Jarrow in 1889 for D.H. Morgan & Co. of Newport. NT 1259 length 240.5 ft. breadth 33.2 ft. depth 16.4 ft.
On 10.8.1904 she was stranded at Briton Ferry, refloated and sold to A. Merveille, France as beyond repair and broken up.

SS Wyndcliffe.
Acquired in 1891, built by Craig Taylor of Stockton in 1889 for D.H. Morgan & Co. of Newport.
NT 1267 length 269.8 ft. breadth 37.2 ft. depth 18.3 ft.
She was sold to W.S. Bailey of Hull in 1892. Later she had Italian, Greek, Swedish and Roumanian owners.
Acquired in 1925 by Greek owners and renamed **Phedon** she was still afloat in 1930.

SS Penarth. (II)
Built by W. Gray and Co. of West Hartlepool in 1893.
NT 2016 length 325.5 ft. breadth 42.6 ft. depth 21.8 ft.
On 20th February 1894 she was wrecked in the Black Sea nine miles west of the Bosphorus whilst on a voyage from Odessa to Copenhagen with a cargo of rye and barley.

SS Castanos. (II)
Built by W. Gray & Co. Ltd. of West Hartlepool in 1893.
NT 1920 length 325 ft. breadth 42.3 depth 25.8 ft.
She was wrecked on 2.2.1905 at the Hook of Holland whilst on a voyage from Rosario to Rotterdam with a cargo of linseed and wheat.

SS Wenvoe.
Built by W. Gray & Co. of West Hartlepool in 1894.
NT 1918 length 325 ft. breadth 47 ft. depth 23.6 ft.
In 1915 she was sold to the Bay Steamship Co. of London.
On 9th January 1918 she was torpedoed and sunk ten miles south of Iles de Glenan.

SS Lesraulx. (II)
Built by W. Gray & Co. of West Harlepool in 1895.
NT 1937 length 325 ft. breadth 47 ft. depth 23.6 ft.
She was sold in 1915 to the Cymric Shipping Co.
On 20.10.1916 she sailed from Cardiff in ballast bound for Montreal and disappeared without trace.

SS Barry.
Acquired in 1895. Built by J. Laing of Sunderland in 1883 for the Barry Steam Ship Co.
NT 1411 length 296 ft. breadth 37.9 ft. depth 20.1 ft.
In 1909 she was sold to N.G. Pittaluga of Italy to be broken up.

SS Westergate.
Acquired in 1895. Built by Short Brothers of Sunderland in 1881 for Weatherley, Mead and Hussey, of London.
NT 1109 tons length 260 ft. breadth 36.1 ft. depth 20 ft.
In 1919 she was sold to Franco-British Steam Ship Company of London. On 21.4.1918 she was torpedoed and sunk 22 miles off Start Point.

SS Penarth. (III)
Acquired in 1897. Built by W. Gray & Co. of West Hartlepool in 1896 for Philip Morel.
NT 1959 length 325 ft. breadth 47 ft. depth 26.6 ft.
On 17th January 1915 she was wrecked on Sherringham Shoal, Norfolk whilst on a voyage from San Nicholas, Argentina to Hull with a cargo of maize. There were only 5 survivors. 22 lives were lost.

SS Parana.
Built by W. Gray & Co. of West Hartlepool in 1899.
NT 1962 length 325 ft. breadth 47 ft. depth 23 ft.
On 5th March, 1913 she was stranded at Montevideo.
She was subsequently refloated and reduced to a hulk.

SS Portugalette. (III).
Built in 1901 by J. Priestman and Co. of Sunderland.
NT 2307 length 339.7 ft. breadth 48 ft. depth 26 ft.
Sold in 1912 to Greek owners. She was subsequently owned by Roumanian, Russian and Greek owners.
In May 1952, her cargo of coal caught fire at Perim. She was unable to make her way to Alexandria and was bought by the British Iron & Steel Corporation for breaking up.

End of Period 2
There were 25 ships in the Fleet at the end of this period.

Period 3. 1903-1919

In 1903 at the beginning of this period the fleet consisted of:

IS Dowlais, IS Cyfarthfa, IS Gwentland, IS Merthyr, IS Treherbert, IS Gardépée, IS Tredegar, IS Jersey, IS Pontypridd, IS Forest, IS Ninian Stuart, SS Collivaud, SS Lavernock, SS Blaenavon, IS Pomaron, SS Hart, SS Westergate, SS Goldcliffe, SS Wenvoe, SS Castanos, SS Lesraulx, SS Barry, SS Penarth, SS Parana, SS Portugalette.

The SS Lyndhurst, although built by Morel Brothers & Co. in 1883, was owned by Philip Morel between 1900 to 1907.

SS Dowlais. (II)
Built in 1904 by R. Craggs and Sons Ltd. of Middlesbrough.
NT 1958 length 330.1 ft. breadth 45.9 ft. depth 22.2 ft.
On 3.12.1917, she was torpedoed and sunk off Cap de Fer with the loss of 26 crew.

SS Cyfarthfa. (II)
Built in 1904 by R. Craggs and Sons Ltd. of Middlesbrough.
NT 1959 length 330.1 breadth 45.9 depth 22.2 ft.
On 11.4.1917, she was torpedoed and sunk 32 miles WSW of Cerigotto. The master was taken prisoner.

SS Cardiff.
Acquired in 1911. Built by W. Gray & Co. of West Harlepool in 1898 for Willie Morel. She was sold in 1915 to R.W.J. Sutherland & Sons of Cardiff who sold her in 1920 to the Sovereign Shipping Co. of Cardiff. In 1924 she was sold to Schulte and Bruns. Germany. On 5.2.1942 she was torpedoed and sunk by a British submarine off Honningsvaag Norway.

No other ships were built or acquired during this period by Morel Limited and at the end of this period the Company owned no vessels at all.

Period 4. 1919-1935

SS. Nolishment. (I)
Acquired in 1921. Built for R.E. Morel & Co. Cardiff by W. Gray & Co. of West Hartlepool in 1915.
NT 2823 length 380 ft. breadth 52 ft. depth 26 ft.
In 1927 she was sold to W.H. Seager and Co. Ltd. of Cardiff 'for about £46,000'. She was subsequently sold to Greek and Panamanian owners.
On 27.5.1959 she was sold to Italian shipbreakers and arrived at Savona to be broken up.

SS. Saint Andrews.
Acquired in 1921. Built in 1914 for Deutsche Levante Linie. Germany as **Neptun.**
NT 3041 length 339.4 ft. breadth 48.1 ft. depth 28.9 ft.
She was surrendered as a prize to Great Britain in 1919 to the Shipping Controller. In 1921 she was sold to Morel Shipping Trust and renamed the **St. Andrews**. In 1925 she was sold to German owners and was interned in Portugal in 1939. In 1943 she was purchased by Portugese owners, who sold her in 1949 to Turkish owners. In 1961 she was sold to shipbreakers and broken up in Greece.

SS. Lesraulx. (III)
Acquired in 1923. Built in 1913 by J.L. Thompson of Sunderland for the Barrie Shipping Co. of Dundee as the **Den of Ewnie**.
NT 2848 length 338.5 ft. breadth 57.4 ft. depth 26 ft.
Sold to Johnson Line of Liverpool in 1916 and acquired from them in 1922 and renamed **Lesraulx** by Morel Limited. In 1928, she was sold to Dutch and later to Greek owners. On 24.10.39 she struck a mine and sank about three miles south of the Inner Dowsing Light.

SS Rhymney. (II)
Acquired in 1922. Built in 1912 for Lunsford Steamship Co London as **Southern**.
NT 2970 length 388.7 ft. breadth 51.4 ft. depth 26 ft.
She was sold to the Holland Australie Lijn in 1915. On Morel Limited acquiring her she was renamed **Rumney**.
In 1936 she was sold to the Guardian Line of which the manager was Alan Roberts, who ran her profitably which Morel Limited had been unable to do, and so impressed the Morel directors that they invited him to become their general manager in 1940.
In 1937 she was sold to a Chinese Company and captured by the Japanese in 1938.
On 17.3.1940 she was wrecked on Luchu Island east of Kumesima.

SS Pontypridd. (II)
Built in 1924 by the Northumberland Steamship Company, Newcastle.
NT 2736 length 399.6 ft. breadth 52.9 ft. depth 24.8 ft.
She was torpedoed on 11.6.42 and sunk by the German submarine U 94 East of Newfoundland.

SS Gardépée. (II) (later: SS Treherbert (III))
Built in 1925 by the Northumberland Steamship Company, Newcastle.
NT 2774 length 399.7 ft. breadth 52.9 ft. depth 24.8 ft.
She was renamed the **SS Treherbert (III)** in 1927. In 1939 she was sold to the Crest Shipping Line of London. On 14.2.41 she was torpedoed and sunk by an Italian submarine.

SS Aberdare. (II)
Acquired in 1927. Built in 1924 for the Cardigan Shipping Company, Cardiff as **SS Merioneth**.
NT 2811 length 400 ft. breadth 52 ft. depth 25.6 ft.
In 1933 she was sold to Italian owners. In 1941 she was taken over by the Brazilian Government and eventually returned to the same Italian owners in 1950. She was sold to Italian shipbreakers at La Spezia.

SS Treharris.
Acquired in 1928. Built by Richardson Duck, Stockton in 1923 for Cardigan Shipping Company, Cardiff as the **Radnor**.
NT 2798 length 400 ft. breadth 52 ft. depth 23.3 ft.
In 1933 she was sold to Italian owners. On 1.7.37 she was wrecked off Castle Point, St. Just, Cornwall whilst on a passage from Bombay to Hull with general cargo.

SS Allende. (II)
Built in 1929 by Northumberland Steamship Co. Newcastle.
NT 3177 length 412.6 ft. breadth 55.3 ft. depth 26.1 ft.
On 17.3.42 she was torpedoed and sunk by German Submarine U 68 off the West Coast of Africa.

SS Nolisment. (II)
Built in 1928 by Northumberland Steamship Co. Newcastle.
NT 3174 length 412.6 ft. breadth 55.3 ft. depth 26.1 ft.
She was sold in 1950 to German owners. In 1960 she passed to Jugoslavian owners and was eventually broken up at Split 26.2.66.

At the end of this period the Company owned 4 ships.

Period 5. 1935-1948

SS Pontypridd　　SS Gardepee (renamed SS Treherbert 1937)　　SS Allende

SS Nolisment

MV Jersey.
Built in 1936 by W. Doxford and Sons, Sunderland.
NT 3032 length 424 ft. breadth 54.2 ft. depth 26.1 ft.
On 28.4.42 she was mined and sunk off Suez.

MV Forest.
Built in 1937 by W, Doxford and Sons, Sunderland.
NT 3027 length 404 ft. breadth 54.2 ft. depth 26.1 ft.
On 21.11.42 she was bombed and damaged by enemy aircraft off Bougie and on 11.12.42 she was bombed and damaged at Gibraltar. In 1951 she was sold to Dutch owners and later to German and in 1968 to Cypriot owners and renamed **Maritsa-2**.

MV Beignon.
Built in 1939 by W. Doxford & Sons, Sunderland.
NT 3004 length 427.6 breadth 56.6 ft. depth 26.5 ft.
On 1.7.40 she was torpedoed and sunk by U 30 in the North Atlantic in position 47.20 N 10.30 W.

MV Catrine.
Built in 1940 by W. Doxford of Sunderland.
NT 3004 length 427.6 ft. breadth 56.5 ft. depth 26.5 ft.
In 1956 she was sold for £465,000 to Transportes Maritimo Atlas SA Panama and renamed the **Tove**. In 1966 she went aground following an engine breakdown. She was found to have considerable bottom damage and sold to Japanese shipbreakers and at Hirao she was broken up in 9.3.67.

MS Jersey Hart.
Built in 1943 by W. Doxford of Sunderland.
NT 4988 length 428.8 ft. breadth 56.5 ft. depth 35.5 ft.
She was sold in 1945 to Stanhope Steamship Co. London and renamed **Standpark**. After passing to other British owners in 1951 she was sold to the Douglas Steamship Co. of Hong Kong. In 1970 she was sold to Taiwan shipbreakers and broken up at Kaohsiung.

SS Jersey May.
Acquired in 1947.
NT 4421 length 423.3 ft. breadth 57.1 ft. depth 34.8 ft.
She was built in 1944 at Bethlehem Fairfield Shipyard in Baltimore USA as the **Samluzon** and chartered to the Ministry of War Transport by the United States War Shipping Administration. Morel Ltd. were appointed managers and they subsequently purchased her. She was sold in 1950 to the Larringa Steamship Company of Liverpool and later to Monrovia owners. In 1969 she was sold to Hong Kong shipbreakers and broken up.

End of Period 5.
At the end of this period the Company owned three ships.

Period 6. 1948-1957

SS Nolisment. MV Catrine. SS Jersey May.

MV Jersey Spray.
Built in 1953 by W. Doxford & Sons of Sunderland.
ESD 9100 NT 3015 length 429 ft. breadth 97.9 ft. depth 26.6 ft.
In 1956 she was sold to the Lyle Shipping Co. of Canada and renamed the **Lake Pennask.** She was sold to another Canadian Company in 1963 and then she passed to Indian, Greek, Somali and eventually Panamanian owners. As the **Lita I** she is still afloat (1979) although laid up.

MV Jersey Dawn
Built in 1953 by W. Pickersgill & Sons of Sunderland. ESD 9150 NT 2879 length 432.2 ft. breadth 57.8 ft. depth 26.2 ft.
She was sold in 1956 to the Scindia Steam Navigation Company of India and renamed **Jalagovind.** She was subsequently sold in 1970 and again in 1975 to Greek owners.

MV Jersey Mist
Built in 1954 by W. Doxford and Sons of Sunderland. ESD 9100 NT 3003 length 429 ft. breadth 57.9 ft depth 26.0 ft. In 1956 she was sold to Sir R. Ropner & Co. and renamed the **Lake Atlin.** In 1960 and again in 1903 she was sold to other Canadian owners. In 1965 she was sold to Greek owners and in 1978 to Chinese shipbreakers and broken up in Shanghai.

APPENDIX 2

Valuation of Morel Fleet

On 3rd June, 1885 Morel Brothers and Company wrote to Mr. Denton the Cardiff representative of Palmers & Sons of Jarrow:

'Dear Sir,

Desiring to know as near as possible the value of the enclosed list of steamers as between partner and partners and as you have had a hand in the building of most of them, it will be easy for you to arrive at a pretty fair estimate without actually surveying the ships which, scattered as they are, would necessitate a long delay. Will you therefore oblige us by giving the value as above and oblige,

Yours truly,

Morel Bros. & Co.'

In addition to asking for this valuation, Morel Brothers also obtained a valuation from Frederick Murrell, Marine Surveyor of Cardiff, on 20th May, 1885.

The two valuations are set out side by side together with the insured value and the figure at which Morel Brothers sold some of the ships on completion to their respective Companies.

The 139 shares in the sixteen ships owned by Morel Brothers and Company, ranging between 1/64ths to 15/100ths, were valued at £26,994. Forty-seven of the shares in Morel Brothers & Company in these ships were, however, owned by M.H. de St. Exupery, a member of the celebrated French family who must have supported the Morels in their early ventures, and his holding was valued at £8,533.14.0d., which was subtracted from the above total.

There remained 92 shares, valued at £18,460, a third of which would represent John Angel Gibbs's holding in these sixteen ships.

In the three totally owned steamers, the SS *Penarth*, the SS *Allende* and the SS *Ninian Stuart*, the value of the 225 shares out of a total of 228 was estimated at £79,185 as against an insured figure of £63,630 and an average of Palmers' and Murrell's valuations at £53,736.

John Angel Gibbs's Executors and the two Morel brothers will have had these figures before them as a basis for working out a valuation of John Angel Gibbs' holding as a partner in Morel Brothers and Company.

Name of Steamer	*Palmers' Valuation*	*Murrell's Valuation*	*Built*	*Figure at which ship sold by Morel Bros. to Companies*	*Number of shares held by MorelBros.*	*Insured Value*
Colstrop	£4,500	£3,100	1874		1/64	£6,000
Galdames	£9,775	£5,775	1978	£16,000	—	£11,000
Beignon	£12,200	£9,548	1879	£16,500	4/64	£17,000
Cyfarthfa	£11,800	£9,200	1880		1/100	£18,000
Forest	£12,150	£9,315	1880		—	£17,000
La Barouere	£12,450	£9,522	1880		1/100	£17,000
Dowlais	£12,200	£9,400	1880		—	£17,000
Lesreaulx	£12,350	£11,094	1881		8/100	£17,000
Blaenavon	£12,400	£11,000	1881		5/100	£17,000
Ebbw Vale	£13,685	£11,320	1881		—	£18,000
Tredegar	£13,685	£11,242	1881		2/100	£18,000
Gwentland	£14,300	£13,540	1882		2/100	£19,000
Longueil	£15,600	£14,881	1882	£23,000	—	£18,000
Portugalete	£14,875	£13,594	1882	£23,600	—	£19,000
Collivaud	£15,100	£13,672	1882	£24,500	2/100	£20,000
Rhymney	£14,450	£13,450	1882	£23,000	10/100	£17,000
Gardepee	£16,825	£16,284	1882	£26,600	11/100	£20,000
Merthyr	£14,875	£12,750	1882	£24,000	15/100	£19,000
Aberdare	£14,875	£12,690	1882	£24,000	11/100	£18,000
Castanos	£16,565	£16,877	1883	£27,600	4/100	£20,000
Jersey	£17,150	£16,020	1883	£28,500	11/100	£20,000
Penarth	£17,400	£16,184	1883	£28,500	97/100	£21,000
Treherbert	£16,200	£16,020	1883	£24,000	—	£18,000
Pontypridd	£17,325	£16,562	1883	£26,000	4/100	£19,000
Allende	£17,550	£16,200	1883		64/64	£21,000
Ninian Stuart	£20,350	£19,789	1883		64/64	£22,000

A comparison between the size of the Morel Fleet and those of other contemporary Cardiff Shipping Firms

	Morel Limited (including other Morel Ships)	*John Cory and Co.*	*Evan Thomas, Radcliffe & Co.*	*W.J. Tatem & Co.*	*Turnbull Bros.*	*Nicholls E. & Co.*	*Seager W.H. & Co.*	*Gibbs & Co.*	*Sir William Reardon Smith & Son*
1878									
No. of Ships	2	12							
Total Tonnage	690	4,457							
Ave. per Ship	345	371							
1888									
No. of Ships	20	17	9						
Total Tonnage	18,803	15,746	9,154						
Ave. per Ship	940	926	1,017						
1903									
No. of Ships	33	20	25	12	7				
Total Tonnage	45,522	33,174	45,864	29,187	12,481				
Ave. per Ship	1,380	1,658	1,835	2,432	1,783				
1908									
No. of Ships	30	22	26	15	6	5	1	1	
Total Tonnage	49,642	36,033	58,515	39,266	11,018	11,992	1,901	2,365	
Ave. per Ship	1,654	1,637	2,250	2,617	1,836	2,398	1,901	2,365	
1913									
No. of Ships	15	20	28	19	6	10	4	2	
Total Tonnage	40,926	56,431	114,292	81,320	19,429	40,228	11,787	7,999	
Ave. per Ship	2,728	2,821	4,081	4,280	3,238	4,022	2,946	3,999	
1926									
No. of Ships	5	10	18	8	2		4	2	36
Total Tonnage	22,945	33,257	84,138	32,542	10,046		16,356	8,711	166,871
Ave. per Ship	4,589	3,325	4,674	4,067	5,023		4,089	4,355	4,635
1936									
No. of Ships	4	3	14	10	1		5	3	29
Total Tonnage	19,140	13,652	72,507	36,642	4,782		21,842	14,330	144,053
Ave. per Ship	4,785	4,551	5,179	3,664	4,782		4,368	4,776	4,967
1946									
No. of Ships	3		5	6			2		22
Total Tonnage	15,300		24,295	26,420			10,792		134,636
Ave. per Ship	5,100		4,859	4,403			5,396		6,119
1956									
No. of Ships	1	2	3	4			1	1	19
Total Tonnage	5,484	13,158	23,870	21,907			7,125	6,314	120,574
Ave. per Ship	5,484	6,576	7,958	5,477			7,125	6,314	6,346

In the 1870s John Cory and Co. had twelve ships to the Morel Brothers' two, but they lost their leading position by 1880 and it was not until 1913 that the Corys again had more and larger ships than the Morels. By this time, both Evan Thomas, Radcliffe and W.J. Tatem and Co. had larger fleets and much larger ships than both the Morels and the Corys and from that date onwards they made but a small contribution to the total shipping registered at the port of Cardiff.

APPENDIX 4

The Composition of the Crews on the Morel Ships in 1885 and 1905

The National Maritime Museum at Greenwich holds the originals for every tenth year or so of the 'Agreements and Accounts of Crew' of shipping companies. Apart from a sample retained by the Public Record Office the great bulk of the remaining records have been deposited with Memorial University of Newfoundland. The Greenwich records were studied for all the Morel ships for the years 1885 and 1905.

These Agreements lay down how the crew should conduct themselves, the scale of provisions, the fines to be deducted for disobedience and drunkenness and any special conditions, viz. 'no spirits allowed', 'the seamen and firemen shall mutually assist each other in the general duties of the ship', 'crew find their own provisions' — which was common on short voyages.

The name of each crew member is listed and the wages, except for the Master's remuneration, are specified. Their ages, county of birth, and town if British, are also noted and they signed their name or made their mark. These Agreements are mostly in force for half a year and are filed under the ship's number in the year that this six-month period ends. Usually there are at least two such Agreements for each year. The Agreements note the port at which, and the date when, the voyage began and ended, and every port of call, where the Vice Consul stamped the date of arrival and departure. It is thus possible to build up a record of each ship's trading in a year. No information of the type of cargo carried is given but this can be deduced from the trade normally carried on from the particular port.

The crews have been listed under the following categories:— men from Cardiff and East Wales, from the rest of Wales, from the rest of the United Kingdom, from Europe and from the rest of the world.

Data has been collected for fifteen of the Morel ships that were at sea in 1885. The Masters of over one-third were Jerseymen, or, if the Masters were not Jerseymen, then the mates might well be. The number of signatures varied from twenty-six to forty, and in one instance a note read: 'The crew shall be deemed complete with twenty-one hands all told'. On some of the six-monthly Agreements there were as many as sixty names entered which indicated a big turnover in the crew and casts doubt on the validity of a simple comparison between the various categories. These are, however, set out below as they give a rough indication of the crews' constitution and provide a comparison with the 1905 figures which are given later.

Signing-on for each six monthy Agreement there was an average per ship of:—

6 from Cardiff and East Wales
8 from the rest of Wales
21 from the rest of the United Kingdom
7 from Europe
(1 only from the rest of the world, a Canadian).

It seemed that those from the rest of the United Kingdom often stayed with their ships for only one voyage, whereas those crew members in the other categories remained longer; so it may well be that the first four categories were approximately equal in size

When a Master was from West Wales a higher proportion of the crew than was normal were also from Wales.

In 1905, there was still a high proportion of Masters from Jersey. Of the twelve ships studied, six had Jerseymen as Masters.

A greater number of Agreements per ship was entered into for this year — four being not uncommon — so there was a smaller number of crew members signing-on on each Agreement. The final figures, adjusted to the nearest whole number, approximate closely to the total crew complement and enables a comparison to be made for this year between the different categories of crew more confidently than from the 1885 figures:—

3 from Cardiff and East Wales
4 from the rest of Wales
9 from the rest of the United Kingdom
12 from the rest of Europe
2 from the rest of the world

The crew members from the rest of the world were often from the West Indies.

The make-up of the crew has become considerably more cosmopolitan between the two years which have been taken for comparison.

APPENDIX 5

The Pattern of Trading of the Morel Ships from 1885 onwards

In 1885, the ships were mostly engaged in the export of coal and the import of iron ore from Bilbao. A cargo of coal was taken on board at a Welsh port and discharged at a French port or a coaling station such as Gibraltar. The ship would then sail in ballast, or with whatever cargo could be obtained, to Bilbao. There the iron ore was loaded, the ship turned around and made the return voyage to a South Wales port, usually Cardiff or Newport. With a quick discharge and taking on board of cargo, the round voyage could be completed within 17 days. The ships could arrive at Bilbao on one day, load the ore and sail the next day; even, very occasionally, they turned round and sailed on the same day.

Longer voyages were made. The ships would sail into the Mediterranean, discharge coal, for example, at a port in Italy and then make their way to a Black Sea port to take on board a cargo of grain, or possibly ore, from Kerch. They would then return to a northern European port such as Hamburg or Rotterdam, or to a port in England, to discharge before returning to a South Wales port in ballast, to take on again a cargo of coal for the next outward voyage.

Ports at which cargoes were taken on or discharged (a sample from voyages made in 1885)

Cardiff	St. Nazaire	Bilbao
Newport	Bayonne	Gibraltar
Penarth	Dunkirk	Santander
Porthcawl	Bordeaux	Lisbon
Swansea	Cherbourg	Barcelona
Briton Ferry	St. Malo	Carthagena
Mostyn	Sables d'Olonne	
	Dieppe	
St. Katherine's Dock (London)	Marseilles	
Glasgow		
Middlesbrough		
Avonmouth		
Ardrossan		
Dublin		
Blyth		
Hull		
South Shields		
Newcastle		

Taganrog	Leghorn	Hamburg
Sulina	Savona	Bremenhaven

Braila	Genoa	Rotterdam
Galetz	Venice	Antwerp
Constantinople	Alexandria	Amsterdam
Kerch	Algiers	

The pattern of trading of the Morel Ships in 1885 is illustrated by details of three voyages:—

SS Forest

Newport	2. 7.84
Santander	11. 7.84
Bilbao	14. 7.84
Glasgow	26. 7.84
Bilbao	2. 8.84
	6. 8.84
Cardiff	15. 8.84
Bilbao	20. 8.84
	23. 8.84
Middlesbrough	4. 9.84
Bilbao	11. 9.84
	15. 9.84
Newport	23. 9.84
Bilbao	27. 9.84
	1.10.84
Newport	8.10.84
Bilbao	12.10.84
	16.10.84
Cardiff	24.10.84
Bilbao	28.10.84
	28.10.84
Cardiff	7.11.84
Gibraltar	15.11.84
	16.11.84
Bilbao	22.11.84
	28.11.84
	11.12.84
Gibraltar	22.12.84
	23.12.84
Bilbao	30.12.84
	4. 1.85
Cardiff	19. 1.85

SS Tredegar

Cardiff	10. 1.85
Marseilles	24. 1.85
Bilbao	8. 2.85
Cardiff	28. 2.85
Gibraltar	3. 3.85
	9. 3.85
Bilbao	15. 3.85
	16. 3.85
Newport	31. 3.85
Penarth	1. 4.85
Savona	14. 4.85
	18. 4.85
Taganrog	30. 4.85
Hamburg	1. 6.85
	6. 6.85
Cardiff	13. 6.85
Genoa	26. 6.85
	30. 6.85
Constantinople	9. 7.85
Taganrog	13. 7.85
	14. 7.85
Rotterdam	12. 8.85
	20. 8.85
Blyth	24. 8.85

SS Blaenavon

Newport	14. 1.85
Gibraltar	24. 1.85
	29. 1.85
Bilbao	6. 2.85
	6. 2.85
Newport	20. 2.85
Gibraltar	2. 3.85
	6. 3.85
Bilbao	12. 3.85
	13. 3.85
Newport	30. 3.85
Gibraltar	6. 4.85
	11. 4.85
Bilbao	15. 4.85
	16. 4.85
Newport	23. 4.85
Cardiff	24. 4.85
St. Nazaire	30. 4.85
Bilbao	3. 5.85
	4. 5.85
Newport	11. 4.85
Cardiff	23. 5.85
Sulina	13. 6.85
Braila	14. 6.85
Galatz	23. 6.85
	23. 6.85
Barcelona	5. 7.85
	11. 7.85
Bilbao	19. 7.85
	20. 7.85
Dunkirk	2. 8.85
Bilbao	9. 8.85
	10. 8.85
Dunkirk	28. 8.85
Bilbao	3. 9.85
	4. 9.85
Glasgow	18. 9.85

1905

In the twenty years that intervened after 1885 Bilbao lost its pre-eminent position as an ore exporting port. Morel ships called there only occasionally. Huelva in Southern Spain on the Atlantic coast and Almeria on the Mediterranean coast shared this role, the latter being the port from which the ore from the Morel mines in the Gergal mountains was shipped.

The great majority of voyages, however, were made to South America, taking out coal from the Welsh ports to coaling stations such as St. Vincent in the West Indies or to South America itself, and bringing back wheat, from Argentina and Brazil to European ports. The ports on the River Plate and its tributaries were opened up to world shipping from the 1890s onwards. A much longer steaming time on passages was involved in the voyage to South America, but the compensating increased rates of freight gave the owners a good return and for many years this pattern of 'coal out, grain home' became the standard run for the Morel ships.

Ports at which cargoes were taken on or discharged
(from a sample from voyages made in 1905)

Cardiff	St. Nazaire	Huelva
Newport	Bayonne	Almeria
Penarth	Dunkirk	San Sebastian
Swansea	Bordeaux	Bilbao
Port Talbot	Marseilles	Lisbon
Barry	Nantes	Barcelona
		Carthagena
London		Aguilas
Glasgow		Castro Urdiales
Middlesbrough	Sulina	Marabella
South Shields	Kustendje	Vila Real
Newcastle	Bourgas	de St. Antonio
Maryport	Varna	Mahon

Rio de Janeiro		Hamburg
Rio Grande do Sul	Naples	Rotterdam
Rosario	Savona	Antwerp
San Nicholas		
La Plata		
Villa Constitucion		

St. Vincent	Santa Cruz	Funchal	Algiers	Oran	Bona	Dakar

The pattern of trading of the Morel Ships in 1905 is illustrated by details of three voyages:—

SS Penarth

Cardiff	19. 9.04
Rio de Janeiro	16.10.04
	3.11.04
Villa Constitucion	10.11.04
	25.11.04
Kustendje	11. 1.05
	30. 1.05
Sulina	31. 1.05
	16. 2.05
Rotterdam	11. 3.05
	17. 3.05
Cardiff	21. 3.05
	2. 4.05
St. Vincent	14. 4.05
	24. 4.05
Rotterdam	23. 5.05
	29. 5.05
Cardiff	2. 6.05
	8. 6.05
Dakar	19. 6.05
	8. 7.05
Rosario	30. 7.05
	14. 8.05
South Shields	29. 9.05
	13.10.05
Barcelona	26.10.05
	3.11.05
Varna	13.11.05
	18.11.05
Bourgas	19.11.05
	21.11.05
Liverpool	13.12.05
Cardiff	18.12.05

SS Dowlais

Cardiff	25.10.04
Santos	23.11.04
	2.12.04
Rio Grande do Sul	8.12.04
	23.12.04
Rosario	28.12.04
	18. 1.05
Cardiff	28. 2.05
	10. 3.05
Rio de Janeiro	7. 4.05
	11. 4.05
Rio Grande do Sul	15. 4.05
	29. 4.05
Rosario	4. 5.05
	11. 5.05
Antwerp	15. 6.05
	27. 6.05
Cardiff	1. 7.05
Barry	5. 7.05
Rio de Janeiro	29. 7.05
	8. 8.05
Rio Grande do Sul	16. 8.05
	2. 9.05
Rosario	12. 9.05
	23. 9.05
San Nicholas	23. 9.05
	23. 9.05
Antwerp	3.10.05
	15.10.05
Barry	20.10.05

SS Blaenavon

Port Talbot	9. 8.04
Santa Cruz	18. 8.04
	29. 8.04
Huelva	3. 9.04
	5. 9.04
Newcastle	23. 9.04
Barcelona	5.10.04
Almeria	14.10.04
	21.10.04
Cardiff	8.11.04
Marseilles	21.11.04
	24.11.04
Cardiff	27.12.04
Algiers	6. 1.05
	9. 1.05
Huelva	13. 1.05
	16. 1.05
London	23. 1.05
Algiers	22. 2.05
	27. 2.05
Aguilas	3. 3.05
Glasgow	21. 3.05
Leghorn	4. 4.05
	10. 4.05
Huelva	18. 4.05
Cardiff	11. 5.05
Funchal	19. 5.05
	30. 5.05
Huelva	4. 6.05
	8. 6.05
Cardiff	21. 6.05
Newport	28. 6.05
Algiers	7. 7.05
	11. 7.05
Vila Real de St. Antonio	14. 7.05
	18. 7.05
Bayonne	24. 7.05
	28. 7.05
Bilbao	30. 7.05
	1. 8.05
Cardiff	14. 8.05

1925 onwards

Alan Hill has described the pattern of trading of the Morel Firm from 1926 onwards:

'When I joined Morel Limited on September 1st 1925 as a junior clerk of fourteen, one of my first jobs was the task of writing out Charter Parties from the River Plate to the United Kingdom or to the Continent for the carriage of grain, and the main trade of the Morel vessels was outwards with coal from Cardiff, Penarth, Barry or Newport, either to Rio de Janeiro, Santos or Buenos Aires, and then either loading a bulk grain cargo for the United Kingdom or the Continent, or loading on the berth from Up River with a parcel of grain and completing Down River, Buenos Aires or Monte Video, with general cargo. This was invariably to London and consisted of dried blood, bones, hoofs, hides, sisal etc., and you can guess that the smell when the hatches were opened in London was far from pleasant.

In the early 1930s, because the homeward Plate market was not good, we took quite a few cargoes of phosphate from Casablanca to South Africa, followed by coal cargoes up the East African coast to Mombasa or Dar-es-Salaam and sometimes to Aden, then worked the vessel from Aden with salt to Japan, thence ballasting down to West Australia to load grain to the United Kingdom or the Continent.

Another trade in which we had vessels employed, some two cargoes per year, was general cargo from London or the Bristol Channel to the Seychelles and then loading guano at Mahe for New Zealand. The SS Treherbert actually took the mooring buoy out from this side and the Master installed it at Mahe. After New Zealand, the vessel would ballast to Australia to load grain for the United Kingdom or the Continent, or for Japan.'

Alan Roberts for the period after the Second World War clarified the pattern of trading of the Morel ships under the commodities carried. Coals were still a major cargo but not only from the South Wales ports. Welsh coal continued to be shipped to Gibraltar and Freetown in Sierra Leone, but coals were also taken from Moazambique to Mauritius, from Hampton Roads in the U.S.A. to northern European ports, from Calcutta to Melbourne, and from Durban or Lourenco Marques to Aden, Italy, Madagascar and New Zealand.

Cereal crops were shipped back to the United Kingdom from Cape Town, Montreal and Australia and also carried to India from Australia and British Columbia, and from the U.S.A. Gulf to Japan and South Africa. Nitrate of Soda was carried from Chile to Alexandria and sugar from Cuba to Liverpool and from Mauritius to Colombo. Imports to the United Kingdom included Sulphur from the U.S.A. Gulf, Esparto Grass from the Mediterranean and Iron Ore from West Africa and the Mediterranean.

'The ships were,' Alan Roberts noted, 'mainly on voyage charter but to get ships out to Australia and New Zealand the Firm aimed at time chartering them to one or other of the established Liner Companies'.

Alan Hill wrote of the 1950s: 'With the new motor vessels we were engaged in quite a few instances from British Columbia and the East Coast of Canada to the United Kingdom with lumber and general cargo, and two vessels on their maiden voyages ballasted out from Sunderland to load in the United States Gulf with soya beans to Japan.

Until the closure of the Firm the vessels were trading world-wide and, following the markets, traded mainly in the long hauls where the best freight rates were obtainable'.

Especially in the later periods of their trading, Morels was essentially a tramp shipping firm, as classically defined: 'owning vessels which in the long run do not have a fixed itinerary and which carry mainly dry cargoes in bulk over relatively long distances from one or more ports to one or more ports'.[1]

APPENDIX 6

Dividends declared by Morel Limited between 1888 and 1948

The dividends declared and the amounts carried forward as passed by the Annual General Meetings of Morel Limited between 1888 and 1948.

They are divided into four periods which coincide with the appropriate chapter headings.

Period 1 1888 — 1903
Period 2 1904 — 1918
Period 3 1919 — 1935
Period 4 1936 — 1948

The Capital of Morel Limited incorporated on 12th May, 1888 was divided into 5,000 shares of £100 each.

Period 1 1888 — 1903

Year	*Dividend*	*Absorbing*	*Carried Forward*
1888	5%	£25,000	£2.035
1889	7½%	£37,500	£4,488
1890	7½%	£37,500	£9,495
1891	5%	£25,000	£1,159
1892	2½%	£12,500	£4,542
1893	5%	£25,000	£7,135
1894	1¼%	£ 6,250	£3,355
1895	5%	£25,000	£1,353
1896	5%	£25,000	£5,626
1897	6¼%	£31,250	£9,619
1898	7½%	£37,500	£4,125
1899	7%	£35,000	£1,607
1900	7%	£35,000	£8,923
1901	5%	£25,000	£5,951
1902	4%	£20,000	£2,559
1903	2%	£10,000	£5,239

Period 2 1903 — 1919

Year	*Dividend*	*Absorbing*	*Carried Forward*
1904	2%	£10,000	£2.481
1905	2%	£10,000	£3,781
1906	2%	£10,000	£2,696
1907	2%	£10,000	£5,327
1908	Dividend passed.		£6,050
1909	1%	£ 5,000	£2,933
1910	½%	£ 2,500	£7,535
1911	1½%	£ 7,500	£7,853
1912	3½%	£17,500	£4,297
1913	4%	£20,000	£11,776

1914	4%	£20,000	£7,035
1915	4%	£20,000	£19,213
1916	10%	£50,000	unknown.
1917	Dividend passed.		unknown.
1918	Dividend passed.		unknown.

Period 3 1919 — 1935

Year	*Dividend*	*Absorbing*	*Carried Forward*
1919	2.48%	£12,292	£14,436
1920	2%	£10,000	£8,855
1921	1%	£ 5,000	£8,805
1922	Dividend passed.		£6,418
1923	Dividend passed.		£3,467
1924	Dividend passed.		£6,702
1925	½ %	£ 2,500	£6,301
1926	Dividend passed.		£756
1927	2%	£10,000	£737
1928	2%	£10,000	£6,231
1929	2%	£10,000	£2,504
1930	Dividend passed.		£8,094
1931	2.2%	£11,000	£3,605
1932	2.1%	£10,500	£2,578
1933	.125%	£625	£2,550
1934	.187%	£937.10.0d	£3,207
1935	.125%	£625	£5,919

In 1925 the dividends were paid 'less income tax at 4/1½ in the pound'. From the 1928 accounts onwards the dividends were paid free of income tax.

Period 4 1936 — 1948

Year	*Dividend*	*Absorbing*	*Carried Forward*
1936	.6%	£ 2,711	£3,431
1937	1%	£ 5,000	£3,544
1938	.125%	£625	£81
1939	.75%	£ 3,750	£1,681
1940	.75%	£ 3,750	£3,623
1941	.75%	£ 3,750	£4,119
1942	2.85%	£14,250	£59
1943	1%	£ 5,000	£2,813
1944	2%	£10,000	£7,171
1945	3%	£15,000	£1,670
1946	3%	£15,000	£6,413
1947	3%	£15,000	£6,235
1948	8%	£40,000	unknown.

APPENDIX 7

Shares and Debentures held by Thomas Morel at the death; valued at 7th October, 1903

Company	Number of Shares	Value	Situation
Shipping			
Morel Limited	2498 £100 ordinary	£60,576	Cadiff
Bute Shipbuilding	1506 £10 ordinary	£12,939	Cardiff
Engineering & Dry Dock Company	100 4½ debentures	£9,750	
Taff Shipbuilding Company	797 £10 ordinary	£7,777	Cardiff
Swan Hunter Wigham Richardson Ltd.	300 £1 ordinary	£304	Newcastle
Sundry Shipping Cos.	43 shares	£1,950	—
Khedivial Mail SS and Graving Dock Co.	200 £5 5½ pref.	£650	Egypt
Coal			
Albion Steam Coal Ltd.	1193 £10 ordinary	£6,710	South Wales
	1143 6% pref.	£9,858	
Cambrian Colliery	21 6% pref.	£179	South Wales
Great Western Colliery Company	40 "B"	£167	South Wales
Locketts Merthyr Colliery	455 £5 ordinary	£2,758	South Wales
	205 6% pref.	£2,216	
	440 10% pref.	£3,217	
Universal Steam Coal Company	195 £100 shares	£15,600	South Wales
	39 £100 B debs.	£3,900	
D. Davies & Sons Ltd.	18 6% pref.	£183	South Wales
	1 £100 deb.	£102	
Iron and Steel			
Ebbw Vale Steel Iron and Coal Co.	1503 £23 shares	£10,381	South Wales
	35 £23 fully pd.	£288.15	
Guest, Keen & Co. Ltd.	100 5% pref.	£556.5	South Wales
Rhymney Iron & Coal Co.	5 £5 "old"	£9.3	South Wales
	150 £5 "new"	£253.2	
Sunderland Iron Ore Co.	60 6% pref.	£135	Sunderland
Railways			
Taff Vale Railway	£7,300 ordinary	£5,046.2	South Wales
	£730 4% 3rd pref.	£828.12	
Cardiff Railway Co.	£3,500 4% pref.	£3,447.10	Cardiff
Rhymney Railway Co.	£2,244 ordinary	£4,151.0.0	South Wales

Cardiff and SW Waggon Co.	30 £25 shares	£150.0.0	Cardiff
Brecon and Merthyr Tydvil Junction Ry.	£500 4% 3rd pref. £500 4% 4th pref. £1000 consol-idated stock	£71.5 £45.0 £55.0	South Wales
Barry Railway Co.	A combined holding of debenture, preference and/ ordinary stocks.	£60,827.2	Barry
North British Loco Co.	25 £10 pref.	£287.10.	
Docks			
Barry Graving Dock and Engineering Co.	14 100 4% deb. 1,083 £10 ordinary 160 £10 5% pref.	£1,323.0 £17,734.2 £1,710.0	Barry
Cardiff Channel Dry Dock & Pontoon Co.	20 £10 ordinary	£195	Cardiff
Cardiff Junction Dry Dock Co.	1 £50 share	£36	Cardiff
Mountstuart Dry Docks	5 £10 pref. ord. 5 £10 defrd. ord.	£49 £38	Cardiff
Tredegar Dry Dock & Wharf Co.	140 £10 ord.	£1,242	Newport
Hills Dry Dock and Engineering Co.	3 £20 shares	£19	Cardiff
Port Talbot Graving Dock and Shipbuilding Co.	500 £10 shares	Nil	South Wales
Buildings			
Universal Building Co. Ltd.	307 £10 shares	£3,070	Cardiff
Bank Buildings Office Co. Ltd	50 £5 ordinary	£150	
Banks			
Lloyds Bank Ltd.	115 £50 shares	£3,593.15	
London and Provincial Bank Ltd.	32 £10 shares	£676	
Penarth			
Penarth Esplanade Hotel	55 £10 ord.	£13	
Headlands Hotel	200 £1 ord.	£50	
Penarth Pier Co.	55 £5 ord. 3 £100 debs.	£32 £300	
Abroad			
Gergal Railway and Mines Co.	14,948 £5 ord.	£9,716	Southern Spain
Transvaal Govt.	£600 3% stock	£591	South Africa
Soria Mining Co.	25 £1 ord.	£25	Northern Spain

Miscellaneous

Western Mail Ltd.	836 £10 ordinary	£6,688	Cardiff
New Cardiff Milling Co.	33 £100 5% debs.	£3,300	Cardiff
	150 £10 pref.	nil	
	150 £10 defrd. ord.	nil	

and small holdings in South Wales Import Co. Ltd. Mordey, Carney & Co. Ltd., Cardiff Grain Co., Davis Stores (Cardiff) Ltd., Metal Mixer Syndicate Ltd., Lipton, Maple & Co., London Paper Mills Co., Western Valleys Water Co., South Staffs Mond Cas Co., Spillers & Bakers Ltd.

The total value of the Shares and Debentures was £267,794.

APPENDIX 8

The Dinner

The Tickets were 12/6 (exclusive of Wine) and the Reception timed for 6.30 p.m. for the Complimentary Banquet to Thomas Morel. The Menu, as printed, and the wine list are reproduced, together with the Toasts and the musical programme.

DINNER
to
THE RIGHT WORSHIPFUL
THE MAYOR OF CARDIFF
(Alderman Sir Thomas Morel J.P.)
Upon his receiving the honour of Knighthood
THURSDAY JULY 6th 1899
TOWN HALL CARDIFF

J.L. Wheatley, Hon Sec.

M E N U

Melon   Fillet Anchovis   Olives Farcies   Lax
Strasbourg Sausage   Cavaire

Turtle Clear

Turbot Mayonnaise   Whitebait Naturel

Sweetbread Cutlets   Mushrooms   Compote Pigeons
Spinach

Roast Fore Quarter Lamb

Spring Ducklings   Chicken in Casselrole and Cress

Pine Apple Souffle   Maraschino Jelly
Eclairs Apricot

Strawberries   Grapes   Apricots   Cherries
Pine Apples

Ice Pudding

Coffee

T O A S T S

1. Her Majesty the Queen
2. The Guest
3. The Mayor and Corporation of Cardiff
4. The Trade and Commerce of the Town and Port of Cardiff

MUSICAL PROGRAMME

March	*"Manhattan Beach"*	Sousa
Overture	*"Tancred"*	Rossini
Selection	*"Belle of New York"*	Kerker
Solo (Cornet)	*"Una"*	Millars
Overture	*"L'Espoir de Alsace"*	Herman
Selection	*"Geisha"*	Jones
Valse	*"Carnival Secrets"*	Tetras
Fantasia	*"Runaway Girl"*	Jones

Conductor — Mr. Fred G. Roberts

Song	*"Rosamond"* Miss Marion Isaac	Chaminade
Song	*"Where's Hugo"* Miss Lal Price	Marzials
Song	*"The Swallows"* Miss Mildred Howell	Cowen
Irish Air	*"Eileen Alannah"* Miss Miriam Jones	
Recit and Aria	*"A fors e lui"* Miss Jennie Ffoulkes	Verdi
Song	*"Summer Night"* Miss Bingham-Hall	Goring Thomas
Song	*"She Wandered Down"* Miss Amy Perry	Clay
Song	*"Calico Dress"* Miss Jennie Ffoulkes	Stanford
Duet	*"Venetian Boat Song"* Misses Howell & Hall	Blumenthal

AT THE PIANOFORTE — Madame Clara Novello Davies

WINE LIST

	Per Bottle
SHERRY	
Amontillado	5/-
PORT	
Grahams — 1887 (Half bottles 3/-)	4/6

CLARET

Chateau Picton Longeville	3/6

HOCK

Marcobrunn	5/-

CHAMPAGNE

Heidsieck's Dry Monopole	8/-
Bollinger	7/-

Spirits, Liqueurs, Apollinaris) 6p per glass
Lemonade, Ginger Ale)

Cigars — 4d and 6d   Cigarettes

Contractors — Fulton, Dunlop & Co.

General Notes

on family letters, minutes of meetings, business agreements and legal documents included in the text.

These are in the posession of the author except for the correspondence with the Dowlais Iron Company, and are quoted verbatim either in full or in part.

The letters sent to the Dowlais Iron Company either by Morel Limited, filed under 'M', or by the Bute Shipbuilding, Engineering and Dry Dock Company, filed under 'B', for appropriate years are in the Glamorgan Record Office.

The Obituaries and news items quoted in the text are from the Western Mail, The South Wales Daily News and the South Wales Echo of the appropriate dates.

CHAPTER 1

1. Joan Stevens, who has revised G.R. Balleine 'The Bailiwick of Jersey' 1970, Hodder and Stoughton, and written 'Old Jersey Houses' 1965 Litho-print & Ashelford, corresponded with the author and information in this chapter and the description of Morel Farm come from these two books.
2. 'Bicentenary of Methodism in Jersey, Channel Islands, 1774-1974'.
3. J.H. Bettey. 'The Island and Royal Manor of Portland', University of Bristol Department of Extra Mural Studies. 1970 p. 21.
4. Robert Pearce. 'Methodism in Portland' Charles H. Kelly. 1898 p. 54.
5. John Angel, Diary fragment, Dorset County Records Office.
6. J.H. Bettey, op. cit. p. 22
7. Robert Pearce op. cit. p.77
8. Sarah Brackenbury letters to William and Sarah Gibbs, 1830-1845, in possession of author.
9. H.C. Mawe letter, 1846, in possession of author.

CHAPTER 2

1. John Davies 'The Second Marquess of Bute', Glamorgan Historian, Vol. 8, Stuart Williams, p. 15.
2. M.J. Daunton 'Coal Metropolis, Cardiff 1810-1914, Leicester University Press 1977, p. 17.

   This is but the first of the quotations from M.J. Daunton's book. It would have been virtually impossible to write such a specialized and 'narrow' book as I have attempted without the wide-ranging and in depth study of M.J. Daunton. Quotations from his book are acknowledged from time to time, but it is his comprehensive work on the development of the Docks and of Cardiff that enables this study to ride, yet able to be 'earthed' when required in the statistics he has gathered, and compared with the trends which he has described from which the Morel Firm departs only occasionally.
3. Patricia Moore 'Cardiff Slums of 1849' Glamorgan Historian, Vol. 2 (1965) Stuart Williams, p. 14i.
4. J.B. Hilling 'The Buildings of Cardiff' Glamorgan Historian, Vol. 6 (1969) Stuart Williams, p. 46.

CHAPTER 3

1. A record of the voyages made by the Gertrude between 2nd June, 1871 and February 1873.

Arrived		Sailed
	Cardif	2.6.71
13.6.71	Bayonne	26.6.71
7.7.71	Bilbao	29.7.71
15.8.71	Cardiff	
	Cardiff	24.8.71
12.9.71	Bilbao	29.9.71
15.10.71	Cardiff	
	Cardiff	27.10.71
13.11.71	Arcachon (Gironde River)	3.1.72
7.2.72	Cardiff	
	Cardiff	19.3.72
24.3.72	Arcachon	14.4.72
21.4.72	Bilbao	30.4.72
24.5.72	Porthcawl	3.6.72
	Cardiff	4.6.72
25.6.72	Bilbao	8.7.72
24.7.72	Cardiff	
	Cardiff	18.8.72
	Cork	
7.9.72	Bilbao	13.9.72
25.9.72	Brest	8.10.72
23.10.72	Cardiff	
	Cardiff	25.11.72
21.11.72	Caen	7.1.73
18.2.73	London	

The only cargo named was the taking on of pitwood at Arcachon.

The S.S. Gertrude sailed in ballast, drawing 9 ft. of water, between Arcachon and Bilboa and again between Cork and Bilbao. There may well have been other occasions when she sailed in ballast and no variation was shown in the log from the 14 ft. of water which was the Gertrude's draft when loaded normally.

For the period when she came into Morel Brothers ownership in 1871, her master was the Jerseyman, John Philip Vallet aged 53 in that year. She sailed with a crew of seven: a mate, a boatswain, a cook and steward and four able seamen. Apart from the mate and boatswain, the crew who signed on at Cardiff for each voyage was different; the great majority were Europeans with perhaps a single Jerseyman, Portlander or Welshman amongst them. The mate and boatswain, too, changed usually after one or two voyages, except for Henry Sansom of Portland aged 59 who served as cook and steward or as mate for most of this period – and beyond. The wages were; mate and boatswain; £4.15.0d a month, cook; £3.5.0d. and able seamen; £2.17.6d. The master provided the food on the prescribed scale. By 1874 the mate's wages were £5.0.0d. per month and those of the other crew members were also increased, able seamen receiving £3.15.0d per month.

The official log books contain records of illness and considerable violence, both the master and the mate being attacked in separate incidents. The Gertrude was sold in the spring of 1875 to R. Dunlop, and Thomas Thomas of Newquay, Cardigan became her master.

2. The Maria Needham, a three masted Barque, 127 ft. long, was bought by Morel Brothers on 25 August, 1871.

On 7 September, 1972 the Maria Needham with William Jenkins, master, aged 43 from Cardigan, and a mate, boatswain, cook and six crew members sailed from Cardiff loaded with coals for Palma. The mate received £5 per month, the boatswain and cook, £4 per month and the able seamen, £3 per month. The provisions were supplied by the master.

After unloading at Palma, she sailed in ballast for Carthagena on the Spanish Mediterranean coast where she took on a cargo of iron ore and esparto grass. She sailed for Cardiff on 12 December arriving at that port on 25 January, 1873, when the crew were discharged and the balance of their wages paid.

On 20 February, she sailed for Lorient in Brittany under a new master, Edward A. Trevis of Portland, aged 31, and a complete new crew, who were paid, generally, some fifteen shillings more in wages per month. She put in at Falmouth where five members of her crew, including the cook, deserted. Between 1 March and 14 March, when she again sailed, five new crew members were signed on, but the cook was not replaced.

She arrived in Lorient on 25 March, but before she left on 5 April another member of the crew named Sophi Demetrios, a Greek aged 22, was discharged. On 30 March, the master noted in the Log Book that he had 'absented himself from the ship without liberty.' He returned on board the next day sick with rheumatism having slept on the wharf and caught a violent chill, saying he was not able to work. On 2nd April, he was still off duty and the master took him ashore to the hospital and left him there. The British Vice Consul found that the grounds were sufficient for his being so left and that no wages were due to him. He further noted; 'that his effects, consisting of one oilskin coat, one oilskin trousers, one bed, one blanket, one pair of shoes and a variety of useless rags have been delivered to me'.

The Maria Needham docked at Cardiff on 18 April.

On 27 May, Edward Trevis and a completely new crew began a long voyage to the coast of the Americas. There were four Welshmen in his crew; Henry Davies, aged 49, from St. Davids, mate, and David Stephens from Solva, John Bowen from Fishguard, and James Williams from Caernarfon.

When they reached Pernambuco in Brazil in September, Edward Trevis was ill with yellow fever and he died at the port. The British Consul appointed Henry Davies, master, in his room and certified that he entered upon his duties on 18 September at the rate of £12 sterling, per month.

Henry Davies was not to be her master for long. The Maria Needham sailed for Wilmington in North America and arrived there early in December. Another crew member was signed on 'for the voyage to Liverpool', but the Maria Needham never made the voyage. She was abandoned between 26 and 30 December; 'by stranding and wreck twenty miles from the port and before proceeding to sea'. The British Vice Consul in Wilmington on 26 December appointed J.H. Langlois, master, in the place of Henry Davies, now mate: the ship could not be salvaged and the Vice Consul noted that; 'the crew members, having been paid their wages in full, had other employment procured for them and shipped in other vessels.'

The documents in the possession of the Firm include insurance policies which valued the Maria Needham at £2,200.

This information is extracted from the Log Books and 'Agreements and Account of Crew' housed in the Library of Memorial University, St. Johns, Newfoundland.

CHAPTER 4

1. B.N. Metaxas 'The Economics of Tramp Shipping' Athlone Press 1971, p. 223.

CHAPTER 5

M.J. Daunton deals with the question of why Cardiff failed to become a shipbuilding centre in 'Coal Metropolis Cardiff 1870-1914' principally on pages 48 to 53.

I have fitted my treatment of 'Morels as Shipbuilders' into his framework and taken the same headings under which to marshal my arguments. Apart from the personal factors affecting the situation at the time, which were peculiar to the Bute Shipbuilding, Engineering and Dry Dock Company, the situations as I describe and illustrate them are on all fours with his arguments.

CHAPTER 6

1. Peter Howell and Elizabeth Beazley, 'The Companion Guide to South Wales', Collins 1977 p. 272.

2. M.J. Daunton op cit p.64.

CHAPTER 8

1. An illustration of the Jersey connection can be found in Lloyds Captains Registers. Captain Elias Nicholas Pallot, born in Jersey in 1847 received his certificate No. 81081 in Plymouth in 1870. The record of his service:—

1870-72	Captain	Eliza & Maria sunk Sept 13 1872	sailing to Brazil
1873	Mate	Bonny Mary	British North America, France, Spain, Portugal
1874-80	Captain	Bonny Mary	British North America
1881	Mate	Colstrup	'Foreign' trade
1882	Mate	Elsie Ker	Mediterranean
1882	Mate	Tredegar	'Foreign'
1883	Captain	Colstrup*	'Foreign'
1883-87	Captain	Tredegar*	'Foreign'
1887-88	Captain	Castanos*	Mediterranean
1888-1891	Captain	Ninian Stuart*	Mediterranean, 'Foreign'
1891-2	Captain	Forest* (collision)	West Indies, Mediterranean
1893-5	Captain	Red Jacket	Mediterranean, France,

(collision) Portugal, Spain

He captained the five Morel ships indicated above.* He died on 15th January 1896. He had settled in Cardiff where his family have remained and his grandson is Glen Pallow, of Glen Pallow and Sainsbury, Accountants, practising at 113 Bute Street, The Docks, Cardiff.

CHAPTER 9

1. Edgar L. Chapell 'History of the Port of Cardiff', Priory Press 1939, p. 121.

Appendix 5

(1) B.N. Metaxas 'The Economics of Tramp Shipping', Athlone Press 1971, p. 6.

Index

Typesetting by Afal, Cardiff
Printed by South Western Printers, Caerphilly
Cover designed by Penknife, Cardiff
ISBN 0 7200 0246 X